Food for Prayer

Claire Benton-Evans

Food for Prayer

Claire Benton-Evans

MINNEAPOLIS

FOOD FOR PRAYER

© Copyright 2008 Claire Benton-Evans.
Original edition published in English under the title FOOD FOR PRAYER
by Kevin Mayhew Ltd, Buxhall, England.

This edition published in 2020 by Fortress Press. All rights reserved.
Except for brief quotations in critical articles or reviews, no part of
this book may be reproduced in any manner without prior written
permission from the publisher. Email copyright@augsburgfortress.org
or write to Permissions, Fortress Press, PO Box 12 09, Minneapolis,
MN 55440-1209.

Cover image: © iStock 2020: Homemade loaf of wheat bread baked on
wooden background stock photo by Mykola Sosiukin
Cover design: Emily Drake

Print ISBN: 978-1-5064-5996-7

Contents

About the author	6
Introduction	7
Daily prayer reflections	
January	9
February	43
March	75
April	109
May	141
June	179
July	213
August	247
September	283
October	321
November	355
December	387
Seasonal material	421
Acknowledgements	439
Sources	441

About the author

Claire Benton-Evans was born in 1970 and wrote her first prayers at the age of eight. She read English at Oxford before teaching English and Drama in London and North Devon. The creative arts inspire her, exclusion makes her angry and family life keeps her feet on the ground. Claire is currently working with church groups to devise fresh, dynamic worship for all ages; this has developed her interest in creative approaches to prayer and praise. She likes empty beaches, good food, live theatre and the Greenbelt festival. She lives with her husband, a Church of England minister, and their three children in North Cornwall.

For the people of St John's, Ivybridge and St Patroc's, Harford, where this book began.

Introduction

This book began with the problem of how to feed a prayer habit. Whether it takes the form of quiet time, a book of prayers or the daily office, it requires time, attention and regular commitment. I ought to do it and I feel I need to, but it is hard – especially when those prayer times begin to feel thin, dry and monotonous. Now I know that how we *feel* when we pray is, many would say, an irrelevance: prayer which wonders, 'How was it for me?' is self-centred, not God-centred; it absolutely misses the point of prayer, which is to enter a place of encounter with God.[1] I know, too, that dryness and dullness can be important elements of that encounter. However, if those feelings turn us away from prayer altogether, then something needs to change.

These prayer suggestions aim to offer some stimulation and refreshment. They are unashamedly eclectic – a magpie's hoard of things which I've found inspiring, moving or thought-provoking. There are prayers which focus on hyacinths, family photographs, Cinderella, the F A Cup, *The Truman Show*, 90s pop music, Abu Ghraib prison, medieval poetry, May Day, ceramic art, windbreaks and *Waiting For Godot*, as well as Scripture, hymns and spiritual writings. Ideas are grouped by common themes and linked to the time of year and Church seasons, so as to encourage the development of a prayer rhythm throughout the year.

However and whenever you pray, I hope that these prayers might help you nourish and sustain your own prayer habit.

January

1 JANUARY

Watching for the kingfisher

> Prayer is like watching for the
> kingfisher. All you can do is
> be where he is likely to appear, and wait.[1]

Is there a right way to pray? How do I listen to God? Do I have to kneel down and close my eyes? How can I stop my mind wandering? What words should I use? Such familiar worries can make prayer feel like a difficult undertaking, but this poem expresses a liberating idea: nothing else matters, because 'all you can do' is sit quietly and wait, like the person on a riverbank hoping to glimpse a dazzling flash of blue.

Whenever you can, find a place to be still and a time to be quiet. Don't worry about what to *do* when you pray: simply *be* – and wait.

2 JANUARY

Janus on the threshold

January gets its name from Janus, the Roman guardian of gateways and beginnings. Janus had two faces: one looked forward, and one back, and we often do the same in this first month of the year.

Pause, like Janus, on the threshold of this new year. Reflect on what you have been in the past, on what you are now, and on what you shall be in the year to come, perhaps using these words of confession:

> Merciful Lord, *forgive what I have been*
> and what I have failed to be;
> what I have said and left unsaid;
> what I have done and left undone.
>
> Holy Lord, *sanctify what I am*,
> touching the best in me
> and healing the worst in me.
>
> Life-giving Lord, *order what I shall be*,[2]
> directing my feet on the road ahead.
> Amen.

3 JANUARY

A gift of bread

Although Christmas is over, the Church celebrates part of the Christmas story – the coming of the Wise Men – at this time of year. It reminds me of a beautiful story for children called *Three Wise Women*. In this tale, three women in different parts of the world notice the new star in the sky. The first is a young woman baking bread, waiting for it to rise overnight. She follows the star and finds the stable, but has nothing to give the new baby. Then she remembers the new loaf she brought with her, and gives it to him. Although he is too little to eat it, he touches the bread as if blessing it. Jesus never forgets this: 'When he grew up, he showed that fresh-baked loaves taste even better when they are shared.'[3]

This story reminds me of the importance of breaking and sharing bread together. When you share a meal today, try saying a simple prayer of thanks:

> Bread-blessing Lord,
> thank you for this meal
> which brings us together;
> bread-breaking Lord,
> thank you for this food
> which is not ours to keep but to share;
> bread-eating Lord,
> thank you for sharing yourself with us.
> Amen.

4 JANUARY

A gift of a story

The second visitor is an old woman who notices the bright, new star as she is telling bedtime stories to her grandchildren round the fire. She travels to find the star and the stable, and arrives with nothing to give – so she tells the baby a story and this, too, leaves its mark on the child: 'When he grew up . . . he told the most wonderful stories to anyone who would listen.'[4]

The stories Jesus told – about silly bridesmaids, conscientious shepherds, lazy servants, truculent labourers, farmers planting crops and working men struggling with debt – spoke to his audience, in terms they understood, about what God's kingdom was like.[5]

In your prayers today, call to mind the many stories we encounter daily: in the news, on TV, in books and magazines and in the stories we tell each other about our lives. Ask God whether he is speaking to you through these stories, and pray for the ability not just to hear, but to listen.

5 JANUARY

A gift of love

The last visitor is a new mother, up late with a teething baby. She has nothing to give but her own child, and she is torn between love for him and for the special baby in the stable. At the last moment, her child stretches towards Jesus and kisses him – and this is the third gift. It makes the deepest impression of all: 'The man whose birth had been marked by a new star taught the whole world that the greatest gift of all is love.'[6]

In a time of quiet, reflect on your own experience of love: the excitement of new romantic love; the deep commitment of a long marriage; the love for our families and for our friends. Give thanks for the love you give and receive, and ask yourself: have I more love to give? Do those I love always know it? Have I denied or withheld love where it could have been freely given? Offer these questions up in prayer, and open your heart to new calls to love.

6 JANUARY
Epiphany

Today is Epiphany, which means 'revelation'. For the Church, it is the occasion when Christ is revealed to the world following the visit of the Magi. 'An epiphany' is a sudden flash of insight and profound understanding, sometimes with life-changing consequences. It feels as if a hidden truth has suddenly been revealed to us, or we have been given new eyes with which to see it.

In your prayers, call to mind those people who are most in need of new understanding, and those difficult situations which are crying out for fresh insight:

>   people whose working lives fill them with quiet despair;
>
>   couples whose relationships are stuck in a rut;
>
>   family arguments which seem impossible to resolve;
>
>   political conflict which has reached an impasse.

To all these tangled lives and mired minds, pray that epiphany may come, as the Good News of Christ came to the world and changed it for ever.

7 JANUARY
Twelfth night

The plot of Shakespeare's *Twelfth Night* is like several pieces of string tying themselves in increasingly complicated knots. Twins are separated by a shipwreck and each believes the other has died. The sister finds work at a duke's court by disguising herself as a manservant; she is employed to win the affections of a local countess for him. Unfortunately, the countess falls in love with her, while she herself has fallen for the duke. Her twin brother arrives separately and returns the countess' love; meanwhile the countess' steward has been tricked into believing that she loves him, and his increasingly bizarre behaviour has led to his confinement in a madhouse. At the end of the play, there is the dénouement (literally, 'untying'): brother meets sister, disguises are removed, lovers find each other and deceptions are revealed.

In a time of quiet, call to mind those relationships known to you which are a similarly tangled knot of emotion, concealment and confusion. Bring them before God, in all their complexity, and place them in his hands. If it helps, tie a big knot in a piece of string and lay it down in prayer, trusting that – however convoluted it may seem – it can be untied.

8 JANUARY
Bad beginnings

There is an annual contest at an American university for the worst opening sentences of an imaginary novel. The entries are hilariously bad, and this is one of my favourites:

> A warning to the reader: Tom dies at the end of the story so don't get too attached to him.[7]

It is kindly meant, but it kills any interest in the rest of the story.

Dreadful opening lines like these remind me of those occasions when we start off on the wrong foot with someone new, or even with an old friend we haven't seen for a while. We may have meant well, but at some point we have all opened our mouths and immediately regretted it – and the memory makes us cringe. In a time of quiet today, call to mind those unfortunate beginnings and offer them to God in prayer. Confess the damage done and pray for guidance in restoring those relationships that suffered.

9 JANUARY
Finding the source

On holiday in Wales, our children played near the source of the River Severn. As they splashed about in the shallow stream, they found it hard to believe that this was the same water that flowed in the great big river we had driven over on the Severn Bridge.

I am often struck by the way you can trace in someone's childhood the source of the adult they would become. The doctor is the child who rescued injured birds and bandaged his cuddly toys; the artist is the messy child who was always painting, drawing or creating something. As a preparation for prayer, consider your own source, and especially the passions, tendencies and funny little ways that you had in your earliest years and carry with you still. Rest in God's presence and reflect on where you came from, and where you are heading . . .

10 JANUARY
Beginners

When I started school, my first teacher had a very appropriate name: Mrs Newbigin. Watching my own children start school, I was reminded of what an important new beginning that moment is in our lives, and of what courage it takes to be a beginner.

As adults, we like to feel we have attained a certain level of competence, and to start again as a beginner – at college, in a new job, as a new parent – can be a difficult and humbling experience. However, there is encouragement in Jesus' words:

> Truly I tell you, unless you change and become like children, you will never enter the kingdom of heaven. Whoever becomes humble like this child is the greatest in the kingdom of heaven.[8]

Today, pray for those known to you who are beginners, that they may be strengthened and encouraged. Pray for yourself, that you may have the humility to be a beginner so that, like a child, you may change and grow.

11 JANUARY

New Year's resolutions

> 9st (excellent), alcohol units 0, cigarettes 29 (v.v. bad, esp. in 2 hours), calories 3879 (repulsive), negative thoughts 942 (approx. based on av. per minute), minutes spent counting negative thoughts 127 (approx.).[9]

Poor Bridget Jones starts her Diary with a long, optimistic list of New Year's resolutions, but by this stage she is reduced to a self-hating catalogue of her failings. It is a vivid picture of what it feels like to let yourself down.

Today in your prayers, admit before God how often you have let him, yourself and others down. Give thanks for the certainty of his forgiveness, which offers us the chance of a new beginning each time we fail.

> Loving Father,
> you know I try
> and you see my good intentions,
> but I find it hard to try all the time.
> You hope for the best,
> though I give you much less than that.
> Help me start again
> when I want to give up;
> help me trust in you
> when I don't even have confidence
>   in myself;
> help me know the power of a new beginning.
> Amen.

12 JANUARY
A new beginning

At this time of year, I am still trying to decide where I can use the many different calendars I have been given. There is the plain, practical one I bought myself; the one with kittens on from my daughter; then the free calendar from the garage and the hand-made ones brought home from school at the end of term. Whichever one I choose, it starts off invitingly blank and full of possibilities, then quickly becomes a scribbled mess of events and appointments.

Today, try praying through action. Take a new calendar or diary and place it, open, in front of a candle. Light the candle and offer to God the blank pages of the months ahead. Let the candlelight glow across the pages, praying that you might carry that light of Christ with you through the coming year, whatever it may bring.

13 JANUARY
A fresh start

There is a moment in the film *O Brother, Where Art Thou* which vividly illustrates the joy of making a fresh start. In rural America during the Depression, three criminals have escaped from the chain gang. They are hiding in the woods when they hear angelic singing and see hundreds of people dressed in white, all moving serenely down to the river to be baptised. When he realises what's going on, one of the criminals wades out to the minister and presents himself for baptism. He emerges triumphant from the water, his face alight as he shouts to his friends, 'Well that's it, boys – I've been redeemed!'[10]

In your prayers today, remember all those who need a fresh start:

> Merciful Lord,
> for the convicted criminal
>   who wants to go straight;
> for the victim, re-living the crime,
>   who just wants to get on with living;
> for the addict who wants to come clean;
> for the separated couple
>   who want to make it work this time;
> for the failed and the fallen,
> for the sorry and the judged,
> and for all of us who get it wrong
>   time and time again –
> may there be the knowledge of your
>   forgiveness
> and the promise of a fresh start.
> Amen.

14 JANUARY
Soul food

> When of your worldly goods
> you find yourself bereft
> and from the goodly store
> two loaves alone are left,
> sell one, and with the dole
> buy hyacinths to feed your soul.[11]

Supermarkets overwhelm us with choice, celebrity chefs tell us how to feed ourselves, and in this market-driven society we are all consumers of one kind or another. In contrast, this thirteenth-century Persian poem considers the importance of feeding the soul. It begs the question: when is the nourishment of our spiritual lives our first priority?

If you have a bowl of new hyacinths in the house, have them near you as you pray and let the fragrance fill your senses. Breathe in the scent of hyacinths, pray for God's guidance, and ask: what can I do to feed my soul?

15 JANUARY

Hungry

When I was at university, African famine was in the news. In order to raise money, the students voted to forgo a week's worth of meals from the College kitchens and eat plain brown rice in the dining hall instead. The money saved from the food budget would then be sent to Oxfam, and we – it was earnestly hoped – would learn something from the experience about the lives of the world's poor. It didn't quite work out like that. After a couple of days, some of us started sneaking bottles of soy sauce and mango chutney into dinner; other people skipped the meal altogether and walked round the corner to McDonald's.

We are not very good at being hungry for the good of our souls. We know how to feast, but apart from some sacrifices during Lent, we have largely forgotten how to fast. As part of your prayers today, forgo a meal or a favourite treat and give up that time to God. Feel empty for a while, and offer up that emptiness in prayer.

16 JANUARY
Thirsty

> It was enough to make me go raving mad. I have never known a worse physical hell than this putrid taste and pasty feeling in the mouth, this unbearable pressure at the back of the throat, this sensation that my blood was turning to a thick syrup that barely flowed.[12]

This is the lone survivor of a shipwreck, describing his thirst after drifting in a lifeboat on the Pacific for three days. It reminds me of a thirsty Jesus talking with the woman at the well. He asks her for a drink of water, then makes an extraordinary statement. He tells her that he brings 'living water', and that those who drink it will never be thirsty again:

> The water that I give will become in them a spring of water gushing up to eternal life.[13]

As a preparation for prayer, recall the last time you felt really thirsty, or pray when you are feeling thirsty. Rest in God's presence and reflect on the other kinds of thirst you experience, remembering that promise of 'living water'. What might this mean for you?

17 JANUARY

Empty boxes

Supermarkets have their seasons and now, after Christmas, it is the season of storage. After selling us more stuff than we could possibly need, they sell us boxes, shelving and storage units to put it all in.

We are all consumers, and we have so much. In a time of quiet today, focus your mind on an empty box or carrier bag in front of you and consider how much of your time and energy is spent acquiring material things. Confess your own temptations and weaknesses, perhaps using these words:

> Living Lord,
> I know the pleasure of a full shopping bag,
> the satisfaction of well-organised possessions.
> I know my head is turned by the glossy
>   promises of adverts;
> I know I focus on the things I could do with,
> rather than the things I can't do without.
> Teach me that the emptiness of this container
>   does not always need to be filled,
> and help me when I can't help myself.
> Amen.

18 JANUARY

The empty bowl

In front of me is a carved beechwood bowl which has never had anything in it. It is too beautiful to be covered up: the wood is 'spalted', its grain threaded with delicate black lines like the coastlines on a medieval map. For years I felt it needed to be used for something, until I accepted its lovely emptiness, just as it is.

In your prayers today, hold an empty bowl in front of you, or cup your hands. That space is open, ready to receive or to remain empty. Simply hold that cupped space before you and rest in God's presence.

19 JANUARY
Overflowing

One of my favourite magical inventions in the Harry Potter books is the Pensieve, the shallow dish filled with silvery liquid in which a wizard stores his thoughts and memories. With a touch of his wand he can extract something from his mind and pour it into the Pensieve for safe keeping.

Sometimes our heads and hearts can feel so full that we need to relieve the pressure. In your prayers today, fill a jug with water and place a bowl in front of you. Call to mind all those worries, plans, hopes and fears that are crowded inside you, then slowly pour them out in prayer as you pour out the water. Offer the full bowl to God for his safe keeping.

20 JANUARY

Emptying

We recently hosted a regular 'Quiet Hour'. There was an open invitation for people to come and sit in front of the log fire together, and simply be quiet. The time was measured by an hourglass, and I often found myself watching the sand at the top emptying itself in a thin, steady stream as the hour progressed.

We may find it in a regular quiet time, a retreat, a peaceful walk or a moment of silence in church: we all need some time to empty out the fullness of our lives, whether they are packed with activity or quiet and care-laden. Today, picture the sand in an hourglass and pray:

> Lord of Life and Time,
> I bring before you my hours and days.
> Grant me some time to empty myself
>   of the worries which plague me,
> of the chores which nag at me,
> of the emotions which shift inside me.
> Grant me some time to empty my heart
>   and mind of myself and let you in.
> Amen.

21 JANUARY

Forgiven

There is a modern poem which wrestles with the generosity of God's loving forgiveness. It is offered to the wicked, the despised and the undeserving, just as it is offered to all of us. The poet vividly describes the experience of suddenly finding that you need this undeserved forgiveness, too:

> ... When you try to wade
> across the estuary at low tide, but misjudge
> the distance, the currents, the soft ground
> and are caught by the flood in deep schtuck,

– only then might you discover that 'God is to be praised' for rescuing fools 'from troubles they have made for themselves. Praise be to God, who forgives sinners.'[14]

These lines highlight the infinite mercy of God's forgiveness: it is mind-bogglingly unconditional. In your prayers, take some time to reflect on the fact that all of us are forgiven in this way. Bring before God everything for which you know you need forgiveness – and those sins which you have not recognised or remembered. Hold it all in prayer and know that you are forgiven.

22 JANUARY
Forgiving

> I have always forgiven those who have
> sinned against me. But I've got a list.[15]

This reminds me of a phrase I first heard as a child: 'He's in my bad books at the moment.' I imagined the 'bad books' as a huge black ledger in which the names of wrongdoers were entered in indelible ink.

Forgiving others is one of the hardest things we are called to do as Christians. In your prayers, bring to mind your own list of the grudges and wrongs you cannot forget. If it helps, make an actual list. As a first step, pray for those who have wronged you – and ask for the strength to forgive them.

23 JANUARY
Not forgotten

A friend once told me she prayed using a litany she had been taught as a child. It ended with prayers for those who have no one to pray for them, and those we have forgotten. This last seemed to be a catch-all, making sure that the prayers left no one behind, out in the cold.

In your quiet time, gather up these forgotten ones in your prayers:

> those without homes,
> those in prison,
> the addicted,
> the solitary,
> the lonely
> and the unloved.

Pray for those who have no one to pray for them, those we have forgotten and those whom we do not know, yet who are known to God.

24 JANUARY
Forgetting

There are things that I know I remember, such as my children's birthdays and where I left my house keys. There are things that I know I've forgotten (trigonometry and most of my A-Level German). There are things that I don't know I remember, like an advertising jingle from the 1970s which someone mentions and I suddenly discover I'm word-perfect. What worries me is the increasing size of the fourth category: things I don't know I've forgotten. I don't even remember remembering them.

In your prayers today, reflect on the experience we all share of remembering and forgetting, perhaps using these words:

> All-knowing God,
> thank you for giving us memory.
> Thank you for these treasure-hoards,
> reference libraries,
> self-help resources
> and home movie collections
>   which we carry in our brains.
> Bless those who struggle to remember
>   but find it difficult;
> bless the survivors who long to forget
>   but can't help reliving horror.
> Bless this complex and resilient faculty
>   you have created in us.

continued overleaf

I praise you,
for I am fearfully and wonderfully made.
Wonderful are your works;
that I know very well.[16]
Amen.

25 JANUARY

Seeing the light

In the Church calendar, this day celebrates the conversion of Paul. As such stories go, it is the mother of all religious experiences. Paul was originally called Saul, and he made it his life's work to round up and arrest Jesus' followers. On his way to Damascus, 'still breathing threats and murder against the disciples of the Lord', a bright light from heaven blinds him and he hears the Lord's voice saying, 'Saul, Saul, why do you persecute me?' After three days of blindness and fasting, his sight is restored and he is baptised. He then begins to proclaim publicly that Jesus is the Son of God.[17]

In a time of quiet, consider your own experience of God. Perhaps there was a flash of insight; maybe there was a sudden change from 'not seeing' to 'seeing' him at work in your life. Perhaps your awareness of him is only just beginning to grow. Pray with thankfulness for what you have received, and open your eyes and your heart for more.

26 JANUARY
David and Goliath

For football fans, January is a particularly exciting month because it sees the start of the Third Round of the F A Cup, when the top clubs join the competition. There is every chance that there will be some 'David and Goliath' matches, in which non-league teams are drawn against Premiership sides. Recently, tiny Burton Albion played Manchester United; Havant and Waterlooville played the mighty Liverpool and – for a while at least – looked as if they might even win.

In your prayers today, pray for all those engaged in an unequal struggle:

>   the victim who names her abuser;
>
>   the whistle-blower who challenges his employer;
>
>   the victimised worker seeking justice;
>
>   the small farmer labouring in the shadow of a corporate giant;
>
>   the protester fighting an oppressive regime.

27 JANUARY
The display of power

At the end of the film *Elizabeth*, there is a scene of transformation. Having battled with her lords, her counsellors and her own desires concerning marriage, Elizabeth resolves that she will reign alone. This moment of decision is marked by her change from a fresh-faced young woman to a magnificent, jewelled monarch with whitened skin, elaborate wig and shining gown. She has become the Virgin Queen.

As a preparation for prayer, consider those who have power over our lives today – not only our elected representatives, but the people who run multinational corporations and global media organisations:

> pray that they might use their power
> wisely, with discretion and judgement;
>
> pray that they might use their power
> humbly, not seeking to exploit it;
>
> pray that they might use their power
> justly, never forgetting their own
>   humanity.

28 JANUARY
Power and truth

In a story of the great Roman emperor, Constantine, there is a scene in which he rests in an apparently deserted farmhouse while on campaign. When he wakes, he is confronted by an old farm steward who takes him for an ordinary soldier. Constantine, tired of being treated with reverence and awe, is excited by the encounter: 'Suddenly I wanted to ask questions of this old man: I saw the chance of honest, even rude replies.' He begins to ask for his opinion, but the old man catches sight of the emperor's purple robe and helmet lying on a chest and prostrates himself in terror. Constantine persists, but realises he has lost his chance: 'When he looked at me I saw the chance of truth gone from his face. Its frankness was drowned in fear.'[18]

Telling the truth to those in power is a difficult and often dangerous thing to do. The prophets of the Old Testament did it, and so did John the Baptist and Jesus himself. The emperor in this story secretly longs to hear the truth, but no one has the courage to speak it in his presence.

In your prayers today, consider those who have power over you, and how you might be called to tell them the truth. Name before God those who are in charge at home, at work, in the church or in the community; consider what is needed, what is neglected, what is done and not done, and pray for the strength to tell the truth.

29 JANUARY

Power and responsibility

Early in the first *Spider-Man* film, Peter Parker witnesses robbers attacking a man who has just cheated him, but refuses to use his new-found super-powers to help. In making their getaway, the same robbers fatally injure Parker's Uncle Ben. Almost the last words he had spoken to his nephew were, 'With great power comes great responsibility'[19] – and so, with this stern phrase ringing in his ears, Spider Man's crime-fighting career begins.

It is a big-budget, computer-enhanced blockbuster – but it is also a coming-of-age fable which underlines its moral several times. It is primarily a lesson for the teenager coming to terms with maturity and independence; yet like all fables it may also resonate beyond the target audience. It may speak to the new parents of a totally dependent human being; to those caring for children or vulnerable adults; and to anyone who finds themselves in charge at work or in the community.

In a time of quiet, bring before God the power you have and place it in his hands. Pray for the wisdom and strength to use that power responsibly.

30 JANUARY

Power and weakness

He came as a King but arrived as a tiny baby born in an outhouse; he moved around the countryside not like a conquering hero with an army, but on foot with a crowd of ordinary working people about him. When he finally arrived at the centre of power, Jerusalem, he quite deliberately made his entrance on a humble donkey rather than a warrior's charger. This Son of God surrendered his power to us and allowed himself to be nailed to the cross – and then triumphed over death itself by rising again.

Jesus completely overturns our understanding of what it means to be powerful, repeatedly challenging people's expectations of a Saviour. In your prayers today, look around you for signs that God's power is working in unusual ways and through surprising people. Pray for your eyes to be opened to the unexpected.

31 JANUARY

Weakness and strength

It is a favourite interview question: 'So, what are your weaknesses?' The right answer, of course, is a weakness that is really a strength in the eyes of a potential employer, such as, 'I'm a bit of a perfectionist,' or, 'I tend to work too hard.'

In a time of quiet, name before God those weaknesses that are harder to admit to. Some may be familiar to those closest to you; some may be known only to you. Some you may try to hide even from yourself. Offer them as channels for God's grace, which works through our weaknesses as well as our strengths. Take heart from Paul's faithful words:

> I will boast all the more gladly of my weaknesses, so that the power of Christ may dwell in me . . . for whenever I am weak, then I am strong.[20]

February

1 FEBRUARY
Knowing

It was like stepping back into 1880 when I visited Lanhydrock House in Cornwall recently. The house is presented as it would have been in Victorian times, and what struck me was the orderliness of life. Every plate, knife and pan in the kitchen had its own purpose and place; every little brass-handled drawer in the Estate Office held papers which catalogued different aspects of life at Lanhydrock. Thinking of the great museums that date from this period, and of Victorian gentlemen collecting butterflies, eggs and fossils, it made me realise that the way the Victorians got to grips with their world was by organising, collecting and cataloguing it.

As a preparation for prayer, consider your own collections. Perhaps you are a hoarder of family mementoes, or your mantelpiece is crowded with photographs; perhaps you have a beautifully alphabetised music collection or an attic full of childhood treasures; maybe you stockpile food or collect china. Whatever it is, reflect on it and what it means to you. Hold your collections in prayer, asking how you might know yourself better through them.

2 FEBRUARY
Connecting

In contrast to the Victorians, we get to grips with our world by connecting – with each other, and with the vast, interactive network that is the World Wide Web. Our mobile phones connect us instantly with other people anywhere in the world, and the Internet has created the social networking phenomena, Facebook and MySpace. Satellite television brings the world's news and entertainment into our homes, live, twenty-four hours a day.

We are used to making immediate connections. In a time of quiet, rest in God's presence and reflect on your own experience of trying to pray. Recognise prayer as a space in which you can step out of time: modern assumptions about communicating and connecting can be left at the door, like a coat. Step into the space and let God speak to you in his own way and in his own time.

3 FEBRUARY
Recognising

Candlemas falls at this time, marking the occasion when the baby Jesus was presented in the Temple. The story is all about recognition. Simeon, an old man, had been promised by the Holy Spirit that he would not die until he had seen the Messiah. As soon as Mary and Joseph arrive with their son, Simeon recognises Jesus for who he is and praises God for him. An old lady, Anna, also recognises him as the Saviour.[1]

How did they know it was him, this tiny baby in swaddling clothes? In a time of quiet, consider this and reflect that the challenge of recognising Jesus is still with us today. He is in each one of us, but it is often hard to see his light. In your prayers, pray for the will to look for Christ in everyone you meet.

4 FEBRUARY

Naming

Naming is a powerful act. When Adam took possession of Eden, the first thing he did was give names to everything.[2] When our children are tiny, we introduce them to their world by carefully naming things: 'Look! It's a *ball* – and there's a *dog*. Now, here's *Daddy*!' In folk tales, a name is a potent weapon. Fairy creatures – famously, Rumplestiltskin – can be overpowered if a human speaks their true name.

In a time of quiet, reflect on those things which trouble your peace of mind. Call them out of their dark hiding places, own them and name them before God, handing them over to him in prayer and subjecting them to the power of his healing love.

5 FEBRUARY
Belonging

Visiting their great-nanny's house, my children were fascinated by the photographs which filled her walls. She is the mother of six children, and they have had children and grandchildren; there were very old photographs, too, of her own mother as a child, and ones from further back still. I was struck by my children's excitement at being part of all this: they belonged to this big family tree.

In your prayers today, consider your own feelings of belonging, reflecting with thankfulness on the family, friendship group, community or club of which you feel a part. Pray too for those who find it hard to join in, who struggle to bond with others or who feel they don't belong anywhere. Pray for an open heart to welcome those who want to belong.

6 FEBRUARY

Footprints

There is a well-known poem about a dream of footprints, in which the dreamer is walking with God along a beach as scenes from her life are shown before her. She sees two sets of footprints in the sand, but during the most difficult times of her life she can only see one line of footprints. She accuses God of having deserted her when she needed him most – to which God replies, 'The time when you have seen only one set of footprints in the sand, is when I carried you.'[3]

In a time of quiet, reflect on this story. Are there bad times in your life that you look back on in wonder, amazed that you managed to cope? Perhaps a current crisis has left you feeling that God has deserted you. Think about that single line of footprints, and take heart: you are not alone.

7 FEBRUARY
The lone footprint

In *Robinson Crusoe*, the castaway lives alone on his desert island for many years before his world is turned upside down by a shocking discovery: a single human footprint in the sand. That unmistakable mark is a sign that his solitary life is about to change; initially he is more terrified than delighted by the prospect, as everything about the newcomer is unknown and beyond his control.

Today, hold in prayer the joys, griefs and challenges of our relationships with others:

> Loving Father,
> thank you for giving us each other.
> Thank you for the wonderful variety of
>   people we share this world with.
> Jesus, Friend and Brother,
> you shared our world of contact and
>   encounter;
> encourage us to reach out to one another,
> and help us celebrate the truth of the
>   other person,
> instead of denying that truth
>   with a label or stereotype.
> Go-between Spirit,
> enable the shy,
> the tongue-tied,
> the frightened

and all those who find it hard to love
   themselves,
let alone others,
so that they may find the courage
   to break out of their isolation.
Amen.

8 FEBRUARY
The human footprint

In these times of environmental awareness, the footprint has become a potent symbol of our impact on the planet. Each of us has a measurable 'carbon footprint', which shows how much carbon dioxide we, personally, have contributed to the atmosphere. This idea of individual consumption was dramatically illustrated by the art installations in a recent National Geographic Channel documentary called *Human Footprint*, described as, 'Your entire life's consumption. In one place at one time'. For example, it showed how many bottles of milk an average person consumes in a lifetime by physically assembling thousands of bottles in the shape of a long pathway which wound into the distance. Such images were beautiful and shocking, and the statistics on which they were based – a baby uses 3,796 nappies; we each produce 4.6 pounds of rubbish per day – were truly humbling.

As a preparation for prayer, imagine a collection of all the things you regularly consume or discard: the fluttering swathe of carrier bags; the mountain of black bin bags; the litres of petrol; the towers of tin cans. However much we recycle, we are all to some extent wasteful and heedless consumers. In your prayers, confess your own 'footprint' on the earth and pray for the will to lessen its impact.

9 FEBRUARY
Tread softly

There is a heartfelt poem in which a lover wishes that he had rich tapestries and beautiful cloths to spread under his beloved's feet. He concludes by saying that, being poor, he has nothing to give but his dreams, and the poem ends with a tender plea:

> I have spread my dreams under your feet;
> tread softly because you tread on my dreams.[4]

When we love and trust someone, we too spread our dreams under their feet. We entrust a friend with a cherished plan for the future; our children confide in us their hopes and ambitions. When someone shares that part of themselves with us, they trust us to cherish it too, and not to stamp on it or spoil it with scorn or negativity.

In your prayers today, give thanks for those who share your dreams and help keep them special. Remember those dreams which others have spread beneath your feet, praying for a sensitive understanding of how you may tread softly.

10 FEBRUARY
Barefoot

St Francis of Assisi walked with bare feet, as a sign of his poverty and humility. An Anglican priest in Shropshire has recently started walking barefoot around his parish, saying:

> It helps my spiritual focus and holds me in the present moment . . . It affects my attitude as I approach life, as each step is different as the foot meets warm or cold, hard or soft, and it reorientates my heart and mind to be ready to meet people with their variety of needs.[5]

Today, as a preparation for prayer, try walking barefoot around the house, or perhaps in a quiet church, or even outside. Your feet are exposed, vulnerable and directly connected with every surface they touch. They are no longer insulated from the reality of the world around them. Hold these feelings in your prayers, and ask God to speak to you through them.

11 FEBRUARY

Lightening the load

Jesus said, 'Come to me, all you that are weary and are carrying heavy burdens, and I will give you rest.'[6] In a time of quiet, consider all those things which weigh heavy on your mind and heart. Place an empty bowl in front of a candle or a cross, and name those burdens before God. If it helps, write them simply on small pieces of paper. Lay your burdens down in the bowl with this prayer:

> Lord Christ,
> help us to have the courage and humility
>   to name our burdens
> and lay them down
> so that we are light to walk across the water
> to where you beckon us.[7]

12 FEBRUARY
Leavened loaves

The Last Supper was the Jewish feast of Passover, and the bread Christ broke and shared was unleavened – made without yeast – because it reminded the Jews of the bread which their people ate on the night they escaped from persecution in Egypt. There was no time to wait for the bread to rise: these were emergency rations made for people on the run.

Unleavened bread was the food of asylum-seekers and refugees. In contrast, the well-risen bread we eat every day without a thought represents the basic comfort and security of our own lives. We live in a place where bread can be made for us, where there is ample time for the dough to rise, where there is more variety and choice in the bakery aisle than anybody knows what to do with.

In your prayers, and when you eat, give thanks for this staple food which we take for granted. Give thanks for the daily bread which we ask for in the Lord's Prayer because it is a basic need. It is not a luxury, and we don't need an extravagant amount, but it is a daily reminder that we have *enough* – and for this we should be truly thankful.

13 FEBRUARY

Living sacrifice

> Almighty God,
> we thank you for feeding us
>   with the body and blood of your
>   Son Jesus Christ.
> Through him we offer you our souls
>   and bodies to be a living sacrifice.
> Send us out in the power of your Spirit
> to live and work to your praise and glory.
> Amen.[8]

This prayer contains an awesome, all-embracing promise. When I was newly pregnant, and feeling overwhelmed by that first-trimester brew of nausea, fatigue, excitement, tearful anxiety and deep joy, the words '. . . we offer you our souls and bodies to be a living sacrifice' leapt out at me: for the first time I knew what that felt like. My body and my life were no longer my own, but belonged to my growing child as well.

In a quiet time, pray through this offering of yourself to God, and ask for God's guidance: what does this mean for you, now? How might your life and work be affected by this promise?

14 FEBRUARY

Loving the unloved

In the film *As Good As It Gets*, Melvin is an 'unliked, unloved, unsettling' man who suffers from Obsessive-Compulsive Disorder but refuses his medication. He is taking his first stumbling steps towards a relationship with Carol:

Melvin: ... My compliment is that when you came to my house that time and told me how you'd never – well, you were there, you know ... The next morning I started taking these pills.

Carol: (*a little confused*) I don't quite get how that's a compliment for me.

Amazing that something in Melvin rises to the occasion – so that he uncharacteristically looks at her directly . . .

Melvin: You make me want to be a better man.[9]

Jean Vanier lives and works with disabled people in his l'Arche communities, which he founded on 'a belief in the value of each person no matter what their culture, religion, abilities or disabilities', and a conviction that 'we are all called to grow in love, wisdom and the acceptance of others'. He writes: 'When we love, we trust and reveal to people their value, their beauty, and their capacity to give life to others.'[10]

Valentine's Day fills the shops with sugary images of romance. In contrast, I was struck by these descriptions of the real experience of love, both human and divine:

it makes us better and stronger people, filling us with confidence and power. Today, hold in your prayers those people you know who especially need that kind of love:

> the lonely,
>
> the depressed,
>
> those crippled by self-doubt and low self-esteem,
>
> the abused,
>
> the addicted . . .

15 FEBRUARY
Spring-cleaning

At this time of year, when sudden shafts of sunlight illuminate corners of the house that have remained cosily dark all winter, it is no wonder I experience an overwhelming urge to give the place a thorough spring-clean. Every cobweb and dust-ball is lit up; even the windows seem coated with a winter's-worth of grime.

In your prayers, look at your life as if with fresh eyes and try to see it in a new light. Are there areas which need special attention? Is there a neglected problem or relationship which needs to be looked at again? Whatever you find, offer it up to God in prayer, trusting that he will help and guide your efforts.

16 FEBRUARY

Cleanse and detox

Celebrity Detox, Life Laundry, How Clean is Your House? – our society seems to be obsessed with cleanliness, if the subjects of many reality TV shows are anything to go by. In the past, cleanliness had a spiritual value – it was, as John Wesley said, 'next to godliness'.[11] Nowadays, it seems an end in itself, as if having a cleansed body and a tidy house is a guarantee of happiness.

In your prayer time, look beyond the cleanliness to consider the way our society is working. Perhaps with a newspaper in front of you, ask yourself: how fair are our workplaces? How just is our treatment of outsiders? How humane is our justice system? How inclusive are our communities? Ask these big questions in prayer, and listen . . .

17 FEBRUARY
Purifying

> Purge me with hyssop, and I shall be clean;
> wash me, and I shall be whiter than snow.[12]

This plea from the Psalms shows the ancient association of sin and dirtiness, and the powerful longing of the sinner to be made clean again. Many religions have cleansing rituals, such as hand-washing and foot-washing, which reinforce this connection between purifying the body and the soul.

In a time of quiet, call to mind all those things which you have done, or which you have failed to do, which have left you feeling grubby inside. Name each one, then offer it to God to be washed away by his forgiving love. If it helps, write your confessions on pieces of paper, using felt pens, and place them in a bowl of water. Handle them as you pray and watch the writing fade away in the water, leaving the paper clean.

18 FEBRUARY

Unclean

Lady Macbeth is famous for compulsively washing her hands. Overwhelmed by guilt for her part in the king's murder, she nightly tries to wash away the blood she imagines still stains her hands. Such behaviour is a familiar symptom of Obsessive-Compulsive Disorder; similarly, people who deliberately cut themselves often find the action a kind of release, as if they are purging themselves of their horrible feelings.

For some people, feelings of guilt or self-loathing are so powerfully associated with a sense of dirtiness that they become ruled by the urge to cleanse themselves. In your prayers today, remember all those who suffer in this way:

> victims of crime who can't stop feeling responsible for what happened to them,
>
> those in the grip of obsessive compulsions,
>
> those suffering from depression,
>
> those who secretly harm themselves,
>
> those who hate themselves,
>
> those who are in despair.

Bring before God those known to you who are suffering in this way, saying for them the prayer of the psalmist:

> Create in them a clean heart, O God,
> and put a new and right spirit within them.[13]
> Amen.

19 FEBRUARY

Clean and unclean

In many African societies, the right hand is 'clean' and used for sharing food and greetings, while the left hand is 'unclean'. In our society, we take a bath to get clean, but elsewhere in the world this is seen as wallowing in our own dirt and showers are preferred. In Japan for example, a bath is for relaxation and refreshment once you are already clean. Jewish tradition forbids certain food such as pork on the grounds that it is 'unclean', but Jesus is understood to have declared all foods clean, saying that 'uncleanness' came from within a person.[14]

'Clean' and 'unclean' are shifting concepts: their meaning depends on who you are, where you live and what you believe. In a time of quiet, reflect on your own views of what – or who – is clean or unclean. Pray for wisdom and insight, so that you may understand how these ideas inform your beliefs, your behaviour and your relationships.

20 FEBRUARY

Creative prayer

This time of year always reminds me of a phrase from a friend's sermon: instead of urging us to give something up for Lent, he encouraged us to take something up; or, as he memorably put it, 'Give vent to your creative bent this Lent.'[15] The following prayers are inspired by this idea.

One of my favourite all-age prayer activities involves salt dough – lots of it. In church, we offer everyone a dumpling-sized piece, and invite them to spend some time shaping it as they pray, before bringing their dough-prayer to the altar. Bafflement and reticence soon disappear as everyone begins to play with the dough, and the offerings are extraordinary: some are detailed, recognisable models; some are beautifully smooth bowls; others have been moulded in response to a particular prayer, and have automatically taken their own, unique shape.

In your prayer time today, take some salt dough, play dough, clay or Plasticine. Hold it in your hands and simply wait. Don't worry about what to say: let your hands do the talking as your prayer flows through you, and let the dough take the shape of your prayer.

21 FEBRUARY
Attentive prayer

I recently enjoyed a walk with a friend whose hobby is textile art. She described the effects she creates by layering scraps of fabric and other materials, and pointed out some mosses which she incorporates into her designs. I had never really paid moss any attention, but in helping her to collect some samples I had to consider the various textures, colours and habitats of the different mosses she required. Some trees were covered in a soft, bright green velvet; some bushes had both a frondy, green-brown variety and a coral-like moss which had a matt, spearmint-coloured surface.

As part of your prayers today, go for a walk and take the time to pay attention. Look closely at the natural world around you: try making a collection of the new catkins, the shells, the unusual pebbles or the budding twigs that might catch your eye. In a time of quiet, use these things to focus your prayers. Let yourself become absorbed in their details and be attentive as you rest in God's presence.

22 FEBRUARY
Caught prayer

Visiting an old church near the North Devon coast, I was drawn to a splash of colour in front of the plain side altar. It turned out to be a piece of old fishing net which looked as if it had caught a multicoloured shoal: tied on to each link of the net were small strands of coloured wool. There was a bowl of extra strands for visitors to add their own, as a sign of their prayer. From humble materials – something washed up on the beach and oddments left over from the church kneelers – had been created this vivid image of prayer: individual intentions were gathered, shared and offered up together in an ever-changing and growing pattern.

In your prayer time, try creating your own tangible prayers. If old fishing nets are hard to come by, try using some twigs in a vase, and use coloured ribbons or paper leaves as a sign of your prayer. Keep your prayer net or tree somewhere safe, and return to it often, especially when praying is hard. Simply add a sign of your prayer, and watch, and listen.

23 FEBRUARY
Active prayer

In our house, everyone's favourite chore is lighting the fire in the early evening. It requires an almost prayerful concentration: you are on your knees for ten minutes, intent on watching a small spark grow as you feed it with kindling and then coax it into life with small pieces of coal. You can't hurry it, because if you simply chuck two big logs and half a scuttle of coal on it, that small new flame will be stifled.

Fire speaks to us in many ways, from the cavedweller's first spark to a lighted candle; from Moses and the burning bush to the tongues of fire which showed the Holy Spirit descending on the disciples. Today, try praying through action by lighting a fire – in a grate, in your garden or in a barbecue. Concentrate on the process of coaxing a blaze from that first, quivering flame and pray as you do so that God might speak to you through this primal action.

24 FEBRUARY

Casting prayer

A recent TV comedy sketch showed a wedding ceremony in a romantic, lakeside location. In the middle of the vows, the bride began to realise she didn't have her groom's full attention; the camera then moved back to show the father of the bride and several other guests being irresistibly drawn to the edge of the lake to skim stones. The groom couldn't help himself, and instead of saying, 'I do', he ran down to join in.[16]

There is something irresistible about the combination of stones and water which could be helpful in prayer. In a time of quiet, bring to mind all those things that you want to be rid of: the guilt, the regrets, the things you want to say sorry for and the things you want to forget. As part of your prayers today, walk beside a stretch of water. Pick up some stones and pebbles as you go, inwardly naming each one with the burden you want to cast off. Hold these burdens in prayer and then, one by one, offer them up to God and throw them into the water. Leave them behind in his keeping.

25 FEBRUARY

Hidden life

> The force that through the green fuse
> drives the flower . . .[17]

Winter has been with us a long time. The trees and bushes have been nothing but bare sticks for months, rattling in the cold wind. Yet it is now that the force of nature is working hardest and most secretly, driving up the sap and pushing out buds full of furled leaves towards the light.

In your prayers today, bring before God everything which feels wintry, dry and lifeless:

- a working life which feels like the same old routine, day after day;
- a home life which feels like nothing but domestic drudgery;
- a tired relationship
- or a stale prayer life.

Trusting that God's power is active even here, make time simply to wait and listen. Don't worry about what to say, or what you need from God: simply offer your time.

26 FEBRUARY
New life

> Now the green blade riseth
> from the buried grain,
> wheat that in dark earth
> many days has lain;
> Love lives again,
> that with the dead has been:
> Love is come again
> like wheat that springeth green.[18]

This Easter carol describes the renewal of life and hope through Christ's resurrection, and the vivid image of strong, green shoots has always moved me. As part of your prayers, go for a walk outside and take time to notice the new life which is budding and sprouting all around you.

In a period of reflection, praise God for the familiar miracle of life beginning again as the year turns; give thanks for the promise of new life and hope for us all.

27 FEBRUARY

New growth

Our garden always looks a mess at this time of year, showing up the inadequacy of our attempts at autumn pruning. Now it needs to be cleared out and cut back to give the new growth some room to flourish.

In your prayers, call to mind the dead wood which is stifling fresh growth and renewal in your life, perhaps using these words:

> Ever-loving God,
> you offer me life in all its fullness.
> Forgive me all the known and unknown ways
>   in which I stifle and suppress this life
>   in myself and others.
> Forgive the old grudges
>   which strangle my relationships;
> forgive the doubts
>   which impede new friendships.
> Take from me all these burdens;
> cut away the dead wood
> and clear away the rubbish in my life,
> so that I might blossom and flourish
>   in accordance with your will.
> Amen.

28 FEBRUARY
New hope

As spring begins to take hold, take some time to gather in your prayers all those for whom finding new life is particularly hard. Perhaps you could plant some seeds as you hold these people in your heart, as a sign of your prayers and a gesture of hope:

> pray for the sick and the dying,
> that they might find new strength,
> courage and peace;
>
> pray for the addicted,
> longing to turn their lives around
> but unable to shake off their addiction
>   alone;
>
> pray for the victims of crime,
> who cannot escape their memories or
>   their fear;
>
> pray for the convicted criminals,
> struggling to become rehabilitated
>   in a frightened and judgemental world;
>
> pray for the depressed and suicidal,
> for whom life has lost its meaning;
>
> pray for people and situations close to
>   your heart.

29 FEBRUARY

Beyond time

This strange extra day gives our calendar a chance to catch up with the precise time it takes the Earth to orbit the Sun. It is a reminder that most of the ways in which we measure time are man-made and self-imposed. We use the calendar introduced by Pope Gregory in 1582 and divide history into Before Christ and After Christ. Jewish tradition counts time differently, compromising with the term 'Common Era' which coincides with Christ's coming, so that 100 BC is described as 100 BCE. Between 1793 and 1806 the French measured time differently from everyone else: after all the bloody turbulence of the French Revolution, the Republic found time to reform the calendar as a symbol of the new social order, renumbering and renaming the months and days, reshaping the week and even remodelling the clock along decimal lines.

In your prayers today, try to think beyond the restrictions of the clocks and calendars which dominate our lives. Surrender some time to God and simply rest in that moment, in the company of the One who is beyond time itself.

Today's entry is for Leap Years only, of course!

March

1 MARCH
Infection

> I came down with an awful virus a month ago that was apparently the same one everybody else had had (fever of a hundred and two, achiness, headache, loss of appetite, exhaustion, depression, a feeling of being *wasted* – a feeling that life is meaningless and banal and the world is stalked by relentless evil and confused by greed and narcissism and that beauty and humour are helpless to rescue it) . . . I felt like death on toast.[1]

We are into 'flu' season now and this vivid description reminds us that illness is never simply physical: it profoundly affects our emotional and psychological well-being, too. In your prayers today, bring before God all those who are ill:

> those hit by a sudden infection who are overwhelmed;
>
> those struggling with a long illness who lurch between frustration and fear;
>
> those in chronic pain who find it hard to be brave;
>
> those close to us whose symptoms we know only too well
>
> and those whose suffering is known only to God.

Hold them in prayer, perhaps using these words:

> Lord, Giver of Life,
> healing is in your hands;
> hold these people close
> and make them whole.
> Amen.

2 MARCH

Sickness

> I am poured out like water,
> and all my bones are out of joint;
> my heart is like wax;
> it is melted within my breast;
> my mouth is dried up like a potsherd,
> and my tongue sticks to my jaws;
> you lay me in the dust of death.[2]

Just as physical disease can disturb our mental equilibrium, so if our mind, heart or soul is suffering we can experience physical symptoms. In your prayers today, remember all those who are struggling with something inside:

> those numbed by shock or chilled by fear;
> those whose panic takes away their breath and balance;
> those whose depression saps their energy;
> those who are dry-mouthed with apprehension or racked by stress;
> those eaten up by a secret or emptied out by despair.

Gather them up in prayer, saying:

> Lord, Giver of Life,
> healing is in your hands;
> hold these people close
> and make them whole.
> Amen.

3 MARCH
Medicine

My small son hates medicine. As a baby he would kick the spoon away, spit it out or scream until he was sick; since then we have tried bribing, reasoning and cajoling, but nothing worked until we introduced the Medicine Hat. This is the silliest hat I could find (a pink and red knitted tea cosy, to be precise), and the rule is that I have to wear it when administering a dose of something. At last, delight at how daft Mummy looks in the Hat has overcome fear of the medicine itself.

In a time of quiet, reflect on those parts of your own life that are in need of healing and wholeness. Consider whether there are some remedies which you resist: is there a difficult conversation which needs to take place, or does a radical change need to be made? Perhaps you need to admit past mistakes and make amends? Whatever it is that is standing between you and healing, confess it before God and pray for the strength to help yourself towards wholeness.

4 MARCH
Recovery

In the first four months of his life, my son had three operations and four stays in hospital. The last operation was the biggest, and he and I were both in hospital for a month. He had been ill all winter, but as spring started to show itself he began the slow but steady ascent towards recovery. Each day, his feeds got bigger and his drug intake was reduced; each day one more machine was unplugged and more invasive tubes and wires removed. A few days before he was finally discharged, the nurses found me a pram and said I was free to take him for a walk around the hospital grounds. It was like coming up for air: my son was getting stronger, the suffocating grip of a hospital-bound existence was loosening and soon we would be going home. I breathed in the cold spring morning and have never been so thrilled to get mud on my shoes, or to see the daffodils' strong shoots pushing up into the sunlight.

In your prayers today, give thanks for the joy of recovery. Praise God for returning those we love to health, strength and wholeness; thank him for the blessing of a fresh start.

5 MARCH

God of the moving image

The Teacher who loved parables understood that dramatic storytelling can tell us truths about ourselves using striking, memorable images. Many of our modern stories are told on screen, and the following prayers are inspired by some favourite moments from films and TV drama.

Indiana Jones and the Last Crusade
A leap of faith

Indiana Jones is facing a series of dangerous obstacles with cryptic clues. He has stopped at a sheer drop, with no way across the wide, dark chasm. The clue tells him to take a 'leap of faith'.[3] He has no choice but to jump off the edge, into the dark. As he does so, the camera swings round to show a sturdy walkway below him, which had been invisible to him as he peered over the edge.

In a time of quiet, reflect on those times in your life when you felt as if you had fallen off a cliff: perhaps a relationship which fell apart; a career path which suddenly came to a full stop; an abrupt and unwelcome house-move; an unexpected diagnosis. Give thanks for God's strong support, of which we are often unaware until we really need it, and gather from this the courage to take new leaps of faith this year.

6 MARCH

The Truman Show
A moment of decision

Truman has discovered that his whole life has been a television programme, and that everything he knows as reality has been carefully constructed: his home town is a set and even his friends and family are played by actors. He has found the door that leads to the outside world; the creator and director of *The Truman Show*, Christof, is trying to persuade him to stay. Standing in the doorway, Truman has to choose between the safe, predictable world he has always known, in which he is the most important person, and the unknown world outside, where anything could happen but he will be free to live and love as he chooses.

In your prayers, bring before God those who face a similar moment of decision, praying that they may be blessed with wisdom, courage and hope:

> the teenager about to leave home to go to college;
>
> those who are leaving a long-term relationship;
>
> those who are about to begin a new life in an unfamiliar place;
>
> those contemplating a major career change;
>
> those who are about to become parents for the first time.

7 MARCH

The Fisher King
Defeating the Red Knight

Jack is a disillusioned former DJ whose talk show unintentionally incited a shooting several years earlier. He has just met Parry, a crazed down-and-out who was once a medieval history professor, whose wife died in the shooting. The encounter has brought him almost to breaking point:

> Jack: I really feel like I'm cursed ... I wish there was some way I could ... just ... pay the fine and go home.[4]

His words show the powerful hold which guilt still has over his life; meanwhile, Parry's trauma has imprisoned him in a twisted fantasy world of medieval terrors. Together, Jack and Parry fight to escape the past and find redemption and new life. This is dramatised as a quest through the New York underworld, in which they must defeat the malevolent Red Knight and find the Holy Grail. The fire-breathing Red Knight who hunts them is a powerful symbol of the guilt and fear which bar their way to enjoying life in all its fullness.

In your prayers, bring before God the 'Red Knights' who pursue you and those known to you. Naming all those things that threaten your peace of mind, open yourself to his all-encompassing forgiveness and the promise of new life.

8 MARCH

Eternal Sunshine of the Spotless Mind
Forgetting

> Oh my darling, oh my darling,
> oh my darling Clementine;
> thou art lost and gone for ever;
> dreadful sorry, Clementine.[5]

A company called Lacuna Inc. has invented a process which erases selected memories from the mind. After Joel and Clementine's passionate relationship turns sour, she has her memory 'treated', wiping away all knowledge of Joel and everything they had shared. Joel tries to escape the pain of the break-up by having the same treatment, but the more it takes effect, the more he fights back. He discovers that he doesn't want his memories, or Clementine herself, to disappear from his life for ever.

If you had access to a memory eraser, would you use it? In a time of quiet, reflect on the memories you cherish, the things you remember that you wish you could forget, and the things you've forgotten that you would love to remember. Lay it all before the loving God who created us and gave us memory. Trust in his purpose, even when remembering causes pain, and place your remembered and forgotten things in his hands.

9 MARCH

Breaking the Waves
Bearing all things

Bess is a sweet, simple girl from a small village who marries Jan, an oil-rig worker. She loves him passionately, and when he is paralysed by an accident on the rig she is determined to do anything she can to restore him to health. Jan convinces Bess that she can help him by describing her sexual adventures with other men, almost as if he will gain strength from her vitality. Bess reluctantly embarks on a series of sexual encounters, and as Jan's recovery falters she is driven to increasingly desperate lengths to do what she fervently believes will save him.

Despite its shocking premise, this film is profoundly moving in its depiction of true love. In Bess' devotion and utter conviction, there is an echo of Paul's famous words:

> Love is patient; love is kind . . . It bears all things, believes all things, hopes all things, endures all things.[6]

In a time of quiet, open your heart to Paul's description of love. What does it have to say to you about your own experience of loving and being loved? What does it say about God's love for you? Rest in silence and let your mind open in prayer.

10 MARCH

Casino Royale
The collapsing mansion

The climactic chase sequence of this film is set in Venice. James Bond pursues his enemies into a grand, crumbling mansion which is undergoing extensive restoration: several storeys of panelled walls, delicate balustrades and elegant arched windows are supported on the water by huge floats and ballast tanks in the foundations. Bond shoots holes in these tanks and, as the fighting rages upstairs, the mansion begins to break apart and sink into the Adriatic.

Not long ago, the sudden collapse of a marriage was vividly described to me in terms which conjured up the images from this film. In many ways, but especially in marriage, we construct and carefully shore up our own shelters against the storms of life, and they can be solid and much admired – but we all have our foundations in the sea. If the house we have built starts to crumble and sink, we flounder, not knowing whether to cling to the wreckage, to swim away in search of dry land, to salvage some timbers in the hope of rebuilding or to drown.

Today, bring before God those troubled relationships known to you:

> pray for those just beginning to build their lives together;
> pray for those struggling through difficult times;

pray for those whose marriages have collapsed. Hold them in your prayers as they face the pain of separation and divorce, or the long, hard job of rebuilding their relationship.

11 MARCH

This Little Life
Hoping all things

A couple's first child is born very prematurely, just on the cusp of life. His mother hardly leaves the Special Care Baby Unit, watching every step of his struggle to survive. Her hope is shown on screen by her fleeting glimpses of a lively, running seven-year-old boy who is the projected image of her son's future self. As she rushes through the hospital corridors to see how her baby has passed the night, the laughing boy skips ahead of her, calling her to follow, promising that there will be good news.

This film vividly depicts hope as something active, strong and very real. The mother's hope doesn't just comfort her, it sustains and guides her. In your prayers today, give thanks for hope:

> Lord of all hope,
> when our lives are emptied out by loss,
> shattered by violence,
> strangled by fear,
> fractured by broken relationships,
> throttled by pain,
> thank you for life-sustaining hope
>   which is always ours,
> even when nothing else is left.
> May those who need it most know
>   its power,
> now and always.
> Amen.

12 MARCH

Quantum Leap
Waiting for guidance

Our hero is a scientist experimenting with time travel. One week he inhabits the body of a cowboy during the gold rush; next he 'becomes' a nurse in the Second World War. In each situation, he must change that person's fate for the better, but his only information about who he is and what he must do comes to him intermittently via his guide, a holographic colleague equipped with an unreliable connection to the experiment's main computer.

How often do we feel this kind of disorientation? We are thrust into new and unexpected situations and try to make the best of things, but we do at least have the promise of a reliable guide, however intermittent and unreliable our attention to his directions might be. Today, dedicate your prayers to listening for God's guidance. Open your mind and heart to all the ways in which he might seek to direct you. Make this a listening Lent . . .

13 MARCH

Bread from heaven

They were enslaved, and now they are free; they have witnessed extraordinary miracles and are being led to their homeland by a man who is directed by God. But after six weeks or so in the desert, all the Israelites can do is complain. They are hungry; they wish that Moses had just let them die in Egypt, where there was plenty of food, rather than leading them into the wilderness to starve. God responds immediately by telling Moses that he will give them meat in the evening and send bread raining from heaven every morning. Sure enough, a huge flock of quails arrives that evening, and in the morning the ground is covered with 'bread', which the Israelites call manna. It sounds delicious: 'It was like coriander seed, white, and the taste of it was like wafers made with honey.'[7] God gives specific instructions that each person should gather only what they need each day and not try to hoard any for the next day, except on the day before the Sabbath when they should gather twice as much and prepare it, so that they can rest on the Sabbath itself. Even these simple rules are broken: some people try to store their daily bread, only to find it goes mouldy; others look for it on the Sabbath instead of making preparations as instructed.

In your prayers today, reflect on this story. Consider how much you have – and confess how often you want more. Pray for the grace to use wisely that which you have been given, and to accept when you have *enough*.

14 MARCH
Fasting

Physical hunger has long been a part of the religious life. It has been used, particularly in medieval Christianity, as a way of subduing the flesh and disciplining the spirit. Fasting may be a mark of penitence or an act of spiritual purification.

Apart from making some sacrifices during Lent, we are not very used to fasting as a religious practice. Today, try to observe a period of fasting, perhaps from dawn until dusk. Think of it not as 'going without', but as having more, because by liberating yourself from the business of preparing, eating and clearing away a meal, you give yourself that precious commodity, time. Offer that time to God and simply rest in his presence, letting him speak to you through your hunger.

15 MARCH

Hungry

> Sixty-five per cent of all North American
>   people are now officially obese.
> Elsewhere, in countries closer to the sun,
> many thousands are still doing the
>   ultimate striptease.[8]

This brutal couplet reminds us of all those for whom constant hunger is a fact of life. Remember them in your prayers today:

> Lord of all goodness,
> where food is scarce and costly,
> and the struggle to survive
>   is hard beyond our imagining,
> help those who have to fight for food;
> provide for those who cannot feed
>   their crying children
> and comfort those who are dying
>   of hunger.
>
> Loving Lord, where food is plentiful,
> heal those who hate their bodies;
> nurture those who starve themselves
> in pursuit of a manufactured ideal of beauty;
> guide those for whom food is the enemy,
> to be resisted or expelled.
>
> For them and for ourselves we pray:
> *Guard us, guide us, keep us, feed us,*[9]
> when you are our only help.
> Amen.

16 MARCH

Basic hunger

One of the many reasons I like camping is the way it re-orders our priorities. Whatever worries have been nagging at us as a family, when we arrive at a camp site with tired, hungry children and stand looking at our patch of grass, only three things matter: getting the tent up, finding some water and sorting out some food. They are basic needs, and there is real pleasure to be had in satisfying them, even if it is only by sitting under a bit of nylon and fibreglass, eating beans on toast, while the kettle boils for tea.

In a time of quiet, rest in God's presence and reflect on your own basic hungers. When it comes down to it, what are the things you cannot live without? Pray for the wisdom to know the difference between what you really *need*, and what you would merely *like*.

17 MARCH

St Patrick's Breastplate
Presence

> I bind unto myself today
> the virtues of the starlit heaven,
> the glorious sun's life-giving ray,
> the whiteness of the moon at even.[10]

The words of this hymn are ascribed to St Patrick himself, and they inspire the prayers which follow, with their distinctively Celtic understanding of God. For the Celtic Christian, the natural world is full of the living presence of its Creator, and its beauty shows us his glory. There is a similar vision expressed in this lovely African prayer:

> May you be for us a moon of joy and happiness... May you be a moon of harvest and of calves. May you be a moon of restoration and of good health.[11]

Like the moon that governs the farmers' seasons, God's presence is real, powerful and intimately associated with the ordinary stuff of life.

As a preparation for prayer, take some time to walk outside and enjoy the natural world. Open your heart to God's presence in his Creation and in a time of quiet, walk with him.

18 MARCH

St Patrick's Breastplate
Connection

Today, science gives us an understanding of our connectedness to the natural world which early Celtic Christians shared instinctively. There is a painting by a biologist called Glynn Gorick, which perfectly illustrates this interconnection of all things. It shows a simple food chain: a heron is fishing for a roach, which in turn eats the *Daphnia* water fleas which feed on algae. Sunlight streams in, feeding the plant cells themselves. What is extraordinary is the way the artist has played with scale to show how all these things are connected. The heron, its fish and the reed beds are painted on the same scale, but where the river disappears into the distance the land becomes a continent half-covered by swirling clouds, as if viewed from space. The sky ends in a perfect arc, ringed with the blue membrane of our atmosphere, and beyond it is star-studded blackness. In the foreground is the view underwater: the water flea is painted in large, loving detail and most of the bottom half of the picture is taken up by a blue-green sphere which is a hugely magnified plant cell, floating like a planet in the underwater darkness. These visual echoes emphasise that the whole of creation – from plant cells to planets – is interconnected.[12]

In a time of quiet, reflect on your place in this richly interdependent world. You are bound to it by the food you eat, the clothes you wear, the very air you breathe. Picture a spider in the centre of her web, her feet poised on each thread; in this way, let your mind reach out in prayer to sense those interconnected threads of the living world which your life touches.

19 MARCH

St Patrick's Breastplate
Closeness

> I bind unto myself today
> the power of God to hold and lead,
> his eye to watch, his might to stay,
> his ear to hearken to my need.[13]

The Celtic understanding of God emphasises his closeness to us in every part of our lives. He is an intimate companion, even in our most mundane activities, and as these words show, his love and strength are with us whenever we need them.

In a time of quiet today, simply rest in God's presence. Know that you do not need to call on him because he is already there, as close as your own breath. You do not have to say anything because he already knows what you need. Come just as you are, and simply be with him.

20 MARCH

The five-stringed harp

Writing in the Celtic tradition, David Adam stresses the importance of coming to know God by using all our senses – by learning 'to play the "five-stringed harp"'. We need to look for God in the world, because 'through our ordinary – God-given – senses the Divine, the Holy Three, seeks out our heart and soul'.[14] The following prayers consider how we use our senses.

Tasting and savouring

> We are so used to belonging to a consumerist society, which gobbles up one thing after another and savours very little.[15]

As a preparation for prayer, consider the things which you have consumed today: not simply the food and drink, but the electricity, petrol, heating oil, plastic bags, toothpaste... In a time of quiet, focus your mind on really savouring something. Remember how good an ordinary bed feels after a week's camping, or how much (albeit briefly) we appreciate electricity after a power cut. Savour something simple today, and thank God for it.

21 MARCH

Looking

It has been called 'the thousand-yard stare': that look which happens when your eyes are open but you don't see anything, because everything behind your eyes is in uproar. Pain, anxiety, anger or despair can preoccupy us to such an extent that we literally cannot see what is in front of us.

In your prayers today, remember all those who look without seeing:

> those struggling to find a way out of debt;
> those trapped in a destructive relationship;
> those who feel imprisoned by their job or their unemployment;
> those who feel suicide is their only option,
> and all those known to you who are in crisis.

Pray that their eyes might be opened to see a way out, a new approach or the possibility of change.

22 MARCH
Seeing

The playwright, Dennis Potter, gave an interview a few weeks before he died. It contained one of the most moving descriptions I have ever heard of what it is like to really *see* something. In his plays, his world-view often seemed black and twisted, but in the advanced stages of terminal cancer he described seeing the blossom on the tree in his garden which he had noticed every spring for years, but which he now knew he would never see again. It became charged with a special beauty, and for the first time he *saw* '... the whitest, frothiest, blossomest blossom that there ever could be'.[16]

In your prayers today, make time to see the blossom and the other delights that spring offers. Take the time to look closely at a flower, in all its intricate detail, or to appreciate the evening sky. Give thanks for the beauty of the natural world and pray that your eyes might always be open to its wonders.

23 MARCH

Hearing

An eavesdropped conversation from the summer of 2005:

Teenager: Have you got these trousers in a size 10?

Shop owner: No, I'm sorry, we won't be getting any more in for a while. Our supplier is in Sri Lanka so we're not going to be able to get anything from there for a bit – you know, with the tsunami and everything a lot of people haven't even got homes, so . . .

Teenager: Yeah, that's really bad . . . So will you be getting some more size 10s in next week, then?

I have always remembered this exchange as a perfect illustration of the difference between hearing and listening – the teenager clearly hadn't taken in anything the man had been saying.

In your prayers today, reflect on your own listening. Are there times when a conversation has merely been two people waiting for their turn to speak? Have you heard a friend talking but not really listened? Consider those closest to you, and ask yourself, how often have I listened to them? Admit before God your own failure to listen, and ask for your ears to be opened to what God and those around you have to say.

24 MARCH

Listening

> She was explaining her program and he was in heavy listening mode, the most aggressive listening the world has ever known: aerobic listening. It is an intense, disconcerting phenomenon – as if he were hearing quicker than you can get the words out, as if he were sucking the information out of you. When he gives full ear . . . his listening becomes the central fact of the conversation.[17]

These listening skills belong to a fictional US presidential candidate, and they remind me of what a powerful thing real listening can be. Helplines such as the Samaritans are founded on the principles of good listening: not seeking to counsel, offer advice or impose your own personality and experiences on the conversation, but simply to let the other person speak, and to *listen*.

I once heard the method for meditative prayer described like this: 'Sit still. Be quiet. Pay attention.' Today, do just that – and during the rest of the day remember that attentiveness and seek to make it the central fact of your conversations with others.

25 MARCH
Touching

Computer technology has brought us incalculable benefits, but it has a major drawback: it allows us to handle life at arm's length. Money is transferred by a few touches on a keypad; relationships are made and broken with the fingertips, via texts and e-mail; a world of contacts, merchandise and opportunities is just a mouse-click away on the Internet.

In your prayers today, consider the disengagement which can result from our misuse of convenient technology. In particular, pray for the casualties of this computer age:

> pray for those who overspend because purchasing is so easy;
>
> pray for those addicted to on-line gambling because it doesn't seem real;
>
> pray for those whose virtual relationships are damaging their real lives;
>
> and pray for those whose only comfort and retreat is in cyberspace.

26 MARCH

Feeling

I used to dread taking my children to houses which were full of interesting knick-knacks. As toddlers, they were always fascinated by these things, but their attempts to investigate were often interrupted by a cry of, 'Oh, don't touch that!' – or by a sharp intake of breath which meant the same thing. The irony was, of course, that my two-year-old didn't want to *touch* the crystal swan, she wanted to hold it in her hands and *feel* it, to get to know it properly by its weight and texture and even taste.

In your prayers today, choose a focus for your prayers that you can hold in your hands and feel. I often use a hand-carved wooden holding cross, which feels solid and smooth in the palm of my hand. Choose an object which means something to you and handle it as you rest in God's presence, feeling its shape and texture. Feel it and know it thoroughly, and as you do so let your mind open in prayer.

27 MARCH
Praying in colour

Colours speak to us in many ways. They affect our mood (greens and blues are calming, reds and oranges make us feel warm) and enhance our language (something sad makes us 'feel blue'). Colour may even be used as a weapon: think of the rebellious teenager who paints his room black, or the American prison governor who makes his inmates wear pink. The following prayers have been suggested by different colours.

Black and White
Colours of certainty

> The message is that there are known knowns – there are things that we know that we know. There are known unknowns – that is to say, there are things that we now know we don't know. But there are also unknown unknowns – there are things we do not know we don't know.[18]

This is an alarmingly honest description of military intelligence, but it is also true for us all. However much we crave certainty in our lives, there will always be a great sea of uncertainty around us. In your prayers today, pray for discernment, so that you may see the difference between what you are sure of, and what you only think you know. Pray for the courage to challenge assumptions and pray for the honesty to say, 'I don't know.'

28 MARCH

Grey
Colour of uncertainty

When questioned about his sexuality, a former Bishop of York famously replied, 'It's a grey area.' This frank response was also a challenge to his listeners to suspend judgement: he was not going to define his own position, so neither should anyone else.

Human beings are driven by the urge to know, and any kind of 'grey area' frustrates us. However, it can also liberate us by giving us the chance to question and explore. There is a passionate plea for this kind of freedom in *The Book of General Ignorance*:

> What we need is a treasure house, not of knowledge, but of ignorance. Something that gives not answers but questions. Something that shines light, not on already garish facts, but into the dark, damp corners of ignorance.[19]

In a time of quiet, pray for the courage to be uncertain:

> All-knowing Lord,
> I find it hard not to be sure.
> I want to know the answers.
> I sum people up before I really know them.
> I would rather sound convinced than look a fool.
> Give me the courage to open my mind,
> the strength to admit to not knowing
> and the will to ask questions.
> Amen.

29 MARCH

Technicolor
The full spectrum

The film *Pleasantville* is set in the fictional world of a black-and-white 1950s TV programme, into which two modern teenagers are magically transported. Life in Pleasantville at first seems perfect: it never rains, the school basketball team never loses, homes are always happy and everyone knows his or her place. However, the modern teenagers begin to show the inhabitants what they have been missing, and as individuals discover sex, or art, or rebellion for the first time, they discover themselves. This is shown on screen by their transformation from black-and-white to Technicolor, so that they stand out as being more fully and vibrantly alive than their monochrome neighbours.

These striking images remind me of Christ's words: 'I have come that they may have life, and may have it in all its fullness.'[20] For some in Pleasantville, this means joyous self-discovery; for others, it means facing their own anger or failure. Life in *all* its fullness means just that: the full spectrum of pain and joy.

In your prayers today, bring before God your own life, now. Whether you feel you are living in black-and-white or Technicolor, or somewhere in between, rest in God's presence, just as you are. Trust that the gift of life in all its fullness is meant for you, too.

30 MARCH

Green
The Green Man

There is a face which can be found in many churches, carved in stone or painted on a boss in the ceiling. It is a man's face, green and half-covered by foliage: he looks as if he is peeping out of a tree or as if his beard itself is made of leaves. He is the Green Man, a figure from folklore and our pagan past whose true identity remains a matter for debate. Some see him as an ancient fertility god or a woodland deity; others claim he is the Spirit of Nature, a symbol of life, death and rebirth which was adopted by the Christian Church to tie in with its central story of resurrection.

As an active form of prayer today, spend some time outside, appreciating the greenness of our world. If you have an old church near you, look to see if it has its own Green Man. As the year's cycle of birth and death turns again this spring, give thanks for the return of new, green life.

31 MARCH

Blue
The Colour of Heaven

This book tells the story of Paolo, a boy in fourteenth-century Venice who travels the world to find the perfect blue for a fresco depicting Mary and the Christ child in heaven, surrounded by angels and saints. He returns with lapis lazuli, a stone from which he and the painter, Simone Martini, make ultramarine blue. This colour was extremely difficult to extract, and thus cost more and was more highly prized than any other. The deepest shades were reserved for the holiest: ultramarine is the colour of Christ's and Mary's robes, the colour of heaven and eternity.

> The people in the painting were stilled, their lives suspended in the great wake of time, rooted in eternity. This was the reward of faith, thought Paolo, an everlasting moment of stability and serenity, unchanging, forever calm, promising nothing less than the certain hope of resurrection ... Paolo handed Simone the bowl of ultramarine and watched him spread eternity over the walls.[21]

As a focus for prayer, find something that is a deep, rich blue: a piece of stained glass, a vase, a clear evening sky or the petals of a flower. Be still, and lose yourself in the colour of heaven. Let the colour lift you out of time as you rest in God's presence.

April

1 APRIL

Temptation

Poverty, chastity and obedience: the monastic vows of the Middle Ages may seem to have little relevance to the majority of us today. However, consider that they stand opposite money, sex and power, perhaps the three biggest worldly temptations, then and now. They are words which shout out at us, as if gold-embossed on the front of a self-help manual about how to 'have it all'. They call to us from tabloids and glossy magazines featuring celebrities, sex scandals, millionaires and royalty.

In your prayers today, reflect on the ways in which you are tempted. Bring before God the small temptations that turn your head and the big temptations that may be starting to control you. Whatever they are, confess them and pray for the wisdom to understand them and the strength to master them.

2 APRIL

Burden

In the film *The Mission*, Mendoza is a brutal soldier and slave-hunter in eighteenth-century Brazil. When he kills his own brother, he determines to repent and lead a new life. He joins a Jesuit mission to a remote tribe in the South American jungle, hoping to earn redemption. As an act of penance he ties the tools of his former trade – all his armour and weapons – into a bundle and ropes the burden to his body, hauling it through the mud, rivers and undergrowth of the rainforest.

In a time of quiet, reflect on your own burdens, particularly those which you have carried with you for so long that they seem part of you, knitted into the fibres of your being. As a first step, try to imagine what it would feel like not to carry that weight around inside you any more; name those burdens before God, and ask for his help in casting them off, little by little.

3 APRIL
Confession

All may; some should; none must.

This neat phrase was used by my Church of England vicar when he patiently explained to me that *everyone* may go to Confession, not just Roman Catholics. Fresh from Confirmation, I was very curious, and wanted to know more: what exactly *happened* in a Confession? I learnt that it was not about being made to feel guilty; rather, it was about unburdening oneself. It often began with an extended discussion and led to a more formal confession, perhaps at the altar. Sometimes there would be anointing with oil, or the laying-on of hands, as a sign of the healing power of God's forgiveness.

Be still in God's presence today and bring to mind all those things for which you need forgiveness. Place in his open hands each burden which oppresses you, and let him bear the weight for you. If you feel it would help, consider asking a priest, minister or pastor to hear your confession.

4 APRIL

Atonement

'A man tries to make amends for his wrongdoing.' This does not sound like a successful pitch for a new TV comedy, but it is the premise for the hit American show, *My Name Is Earl*. Earl is a thief and lifelong ne'er-do-well who becomes convinced that bad things keep happening to him because of all the bad things he has done to others. He is determined to put things right, and starts by compiling an enormous list of everything he ever did wrong. Item by item, he works his way down the list, trying to make things better by revisiting all the angry people, awkward situations and messed-up lives he had left in his wake. As he says, 'I'm just trying to be a better person.'[1]

In a time of quiet, bring before God those things which you feel bad about. Open your mind to the possibility of helping to make amends; pray for the courage to make things better, and the wisdom to know what to do.

5 APRIL

God on the streets

The following prayers are inspired by the Manchester Passion of 2006, in which the Easter story was told in the streets of Manchester, and powerfully expressed through the music of Mancunian pop groups. The disciples were young men in hoodies, the soldiers were riot police and Jesus, condemned to die, was dressed in an orange jumpsuit, his head covered by a bag. In this context, the modern secular songs spoke with heartfelt directness about human encounters with Christ.

'Love Will Tear Us Apart'

When love, love will tear us apart again.[2]

Jesus sang this at the Last Supper, when he predicted his betrayal and death. The words brought home to me the intimacy of that event: it is a special meal shared among close friends. The pain Jesus will endure is not just physical. He will be betrayed and denied by his best friends, then torn away from them.

In a time of quiet, pray for all those who are suffering emotional pain: the bereaved, the guilty, those whose marriages have broken down, the depressed, the lonely, the despairing . . .

6 APRIL

'Sit Down'

> Those who feel the breath of sadness,
> sit down next to me;
> those who find they're touched by
>   madness,
> sit down next to me;
> those who find themselves ridiculous,
> sit down next to me;
> in love, in fear, in hate, in tears . . .
> sit down next to me.[3]

Jesus sang this in the Garden of Gethsemane, and his words seemed to appeal to all of us, not just the sleeping disciples. Christ's invitation here is utterly all-embracing: come to me, whoever and whatever you are. His love includes us all: the sad and the mad, the meek and those who mourn, those who can't even love themselves.

In your prayers this week, give thanks for this wonderful love, which is always on offer to us. Pray too for guidance in following Christ's example. We are called to sit down, as he did, next to our fellow human beings, in all their variety. Ask for new eyes to see those whom we have excluded, and a new resolve to include them.

7 APRIL
'Blue Monday'

> How does it feel to treat me like you do?
> When you've your hands upon me
> and told me who you are.
> I thought I was mistaken,
> I thought I heard your words . . .
> tell me now, how do I feel?[4]

Judas sang this to Jesus when he turned him over to the soldiers in the Garden of Gethsemane. His words expressed his own sense of betrayal: Jesus was not the leader Judas thought he was.

We can often be misled by others and by our own misconceptions into forming a mistaken understanding of who God is and what he wants from us. In your prayers, open your mind and heart to the possibility of a fresh encounter with God which will set you back on the right path. It might come through another person, something read or seen, or through a new experience of prayer or worship. Pray that you might feel God's hands upon you.

8 APRIL

'Wonderwall'

> And all the roads we have to walk along
>   are winding,
> and all the lights that lead us there are
>   blinding;
> there are many things that I would
>   like to say to you,
> but I don't know how.[5]

Pilate sang these words to Christ, a baffled response to the silent figure before him.

In your prayers today, resist the temptation to bombard God with all the things you want to say. Try simply to rest in silence and listen instead. Step aside from those busy roads we have to walk; turn away from all those things which clamour for our attention and lead us in different directions: be still, and listen to what God has to say to you.

9 APRIL
Home

Imagine coming home one night with your family and finding that everything in your house has been taken. Not just the TV and the stereo, but the carpets, the toilet rolls and the hooks for your coats. That is the premise for Alan Bennett's story, *The Clothes They Stood Up In*. It explores the effect of such a comprehensive burglary on a prosperous middle-class couple, Mr and Mrs Ransome:

> What she did miss – and this was harder to put into words – was not so much the things themselves as her particular paths through them. There was the green bobble hat she had had, for instance, which she never actually wore but would always put on the hall table to remind her that she had switched the immersion heater on in the bathroom ... But with no bobble hat she'd twice left the immersion on all night and once Mr Ransome had scalded his hand.[6]

In your prayers today, walk around your home and appreciate the little things that make it familiar. Take some time to thank God for these everyday comforts, perhaps using these words:

> We bless you for the chance to be ourselves,
> for the tasks that weave the pattern of our days,
> for the sweet, familiar round of ordinary
>   things.
> Blessed are you, strong, sheltering God.[7]

10 APRIL

House-bound

'Home is where the hurt is.' This memorable phrase, used in campaigns against both domestic violence and child abuse, reminds us that home is not a refuge for everyone.

In your prayers today, remember those for whom 'home' means fear, danger or a suffocating sense of confinement.

> God of shelter,
> bless those whose home is a prison
> of domestic violence or abuse,
> of family breakdown,
> of illness or addiction,
> of old age and infirmity,
> of unemployment and despair.
>
> God of refuge,
> lead those who suffer to a safe place,
> to healing and wholeness,
> to peace and the possibility of a fresh
>   start.
>
> God of strength,
> support those who feel weak,
> encourage those who feel trapped
> and empower all who help them.
> Amen.

11 APRIL

Insiders and outsiders

The story of *Oryx and Crake*[8] is set in a monstrous world of the future, in which climate change and genetic modification have altered life almost beyond recognition. The world's population is divided: those involved in scientific research live with their families in sealed towns with heavily guarded perimeters, called the Compounds; the rest live in the Pleeblands, the lawless wilderness outside. Families transfer between Compounds in sealed trains, and young men who visit the Pleeblands to walk on the wild side, protect themselves first with an intravenous shot of powerful compound antibiotics.

In a time of quiet, reflect on this vision of the future. Bring before God the no-go areas in our own world:

> the sink estates,
> the downtown streets,
> the failing schools,
> the inner-city tower blocks,
> the dying rural communities.

Whether they are a remote concern or a pressing problem in your life, hold them together in prayer.

12 APRIL

Outside the city walls

Towns and cities, especially Roman ones, used to be built with encircling walls to protect them from attack. Today, there is renewed interest in building 'gated communities': in parts of South Africa and the United States such places are well established, and access is strictly controlled by security guards and passes. In this country, locked gates are being installed at the ends of back street alleys, for example in inner-city Plymouth, in an attempt to tackle the problems of litter, vandalism and drug abuse in the alleyways.

As a preparation for prayer, make a circle around you with a line or a long piece of string. In a time of quiet, reflect on your feelings within that circle, where the space is yours, and think of those parts of your life that are inside that circle. Then ask God to lead you outside your boundary fence, and open your eyes to those people and situations which you do not include in your life. For yourself and others, say the following prayer:

> *For those happy in their cosy circle of family*
>   *and friends*
> *who do not want that circle pulled out of shape*
>   *by reaching out to the lonely and outcast*[9],
>   I pray:
> Loving Lord, your hands touched, included
>   and shared;
> show us all how to reach out to the
>   excluded with your touch.
> Amen.

13 APRIL
Exiles

In the past, communities meted out a simple form of justice: severe wrongdoing was punished by death or exile. Unacceptable behaviour put a person literally 'beyond the pale' – that is, outside the fence. Today, exile is often the fate of victims, the dispossessed, the poor and the marginalised, as shown by these bitter words from a charity's appeal leaflet:

> The desert outside Darfur's refugee camps
> is a vicious, lawless, no man's land.
> Just as well it's only women and children
> who have to come here.[10]

In your prayers, remember those suffering in exile today:

> pray for the refugees and asylum-seekers,
> made homeless by war, genocide or
>   natural disaster;
>
> pray for those in our own towns and villages,
> exiled from the community they grew up in
> by inflated house-prices and unemployment;
>
> pray for those children excluded from
>   school whose prospects are bleak;
>
> pray for those whose actions, beliefs or
>   way of life have made them social
>   outcasts;
>
> pray for all those known to you who are
>   exiled
> and those whose exclusion is known only
>   to God.

14 APRIL

Homecoming

The wild child of the family had run away. He took his half of the inheritance then disappeared and went travelling. The money all went on drink, drugs and gambling and soon he had nothing left. He was in a poor country which was suffering from severe food shortages, and the only work he could find was casual labour on a pig farm. He fed the pigs, but there was nothing spare for him to eat. Finally, half-dead from malnutrition, he remembered the farm where he had grown up and drooled at the memory of the huge hunks of bread the farmhands ate in the fields. He made his way home, determined to admit how stupid he had been and to beg for work as a farm labourer. But he was completely unprepared for what happened: his father ran to meet him, folded him in his arms and kissed him. Then he threw a big party in his honour.

This Parable of the Prodigal Son[11] gives us one of the most moving descriptions of homecoming I know. The son who, through his own fault, had nothing left receives everything: open arms, complete forgiveness – and the best clothes and a big feast.

In your prayers today, consider your own home and family, the community in which you have put down roots, the loving relationships you share and everything which gives you the satisfaction, fulfilment and deep happiness which can best be summed up by the words, 'It feels like coming home.' Name them before God and give thanks for the joy of homecoming.

15 APRIL

Pilgrimage

In the Middle Ages, April was the time for going on a pilgrimage to a holy place – to one of the great churches of Europe, to Jerusalem itself or, in the case of Chaucer's storytelling pilgrims, to Canterbury Cathedral. A couple of years ago, the vicar of a church in Devon named after St Petroc, the Cornish saint, organised a pilgrimage from St Petroc's Church in Dartmouth to St Petroc's Church in Padstow, taking in a string of other churches with the same patron saint along the way. The route took them across the rough heights of Dartmoor, past the prison, through the tangled depths of ancient woodland and down the path of the old railway beside the River Camel. At the brief service of celebration – and rather longer cream tea – in the Padstow church, I was struck by how well the pilgrims looked. They were sunburnt and blistered, but they were full of a sense of achievement, having come all that way, got lost, broken a boot on the moor, had a mystical encounter with a lone white horse, told jokes, talked and walked.

Today, try an active form of prayer and make a pilgrimage of your own. Choose a place that means something to you and make your way there. On your journey, let your mind relax and open in prayer, and let the act of pilgrimage speak to you.

16 APRIL

Pilgrims and settlers

Jesus issued a challenge to all of us to become pilgrims on the road with him. A good, religious man once asked him what more he had to do to inherit eternal life:

> Jesus, looking at him, loved him and said, 'You lack one thing; go, sell what you own, and give the money to the poor, and you will have treasure in heaven; then come, follow me.' When he heard this, he was shocked and went away grieving, for he had many possessions.[12]

The answer is straightforward and gently spoken but uncompromising. Who can blame the man for his reaction? Following the Way as pilgrims, rather than settlers, is an appealing idea, but how do we really become pilgrims with mortgages, debts, children in school or dependent parents? How can we sell all we have when our family still needs food on the table and somewhere to sleep?

In a time of quiet, bring these questions, and questions of your own, to God in prayer. Rest in his presence and trust in his wisdom and guidance. The answers may be a long time in coming, and may come in unexpected ways. Take the time today simply to ask questions, and wait . . .

17 APRIL

Easter Garden

My children love helping to make the Easter Garden in church. They get to mould piles of soil into hills, make a patchwork of green felt and astro-turf and construct a tomb out of stones and pebbles. I am always impressed by their care and attentiveness: it looks like prayer in action. This year, they arranged spring flowers to form patterns on saucers and fountains in tiny glass vases. Then they made a pathway of flat stones leading to the tomb, and placed a small, smooth, heart-shaped piece of slate directly outside the entrance. In the tomb itself, surrounding a tea-light, they placed sprigs of rosemary, just as the women took spices to anoint Christ's body.

Today, make your own prayer by collecting and arranging some things that speak to you of Easter. If you have children or grandchildren, try making an Easter garden together. Alternatively, you could make your own arrangement of candles, spring herbs, wild flowers, water, wine or a hammer and nails. Whatever you make, place it where it won't be disturbed and use it as a focus for prayer during this Easter season.

18 APRIL

Beating the bounds

It is still the practice in many churches to walk in a procession around the boundary of the parish at this time of year, known as 'beating the bounds'. God's blessing is asked on the land within the bounds; in rural parishes, crops are blessed. In my husband's last parish, he and his churchwarden found themselves, fully robed and carrying a large cross, in a field full of rather skittish cows. The landowner was a redoubtable woman in her eighties, and when my husband pointed out that they were about to process through her stock, she replied, 'Course you are! Why do you think I want these fields blessed?' The next field was even trickier: it contained Curly, the bull. His owner advised, 'If Curly gets a bit frisky, whack him with the cross!'

Today, try an active form of prayer. Walk the boundary of your property, parish, town or community, picturing a boundary line as you do so. Pray for God's blessing on all those inside: those known to you and those who are strangers; those who are well established and those who are just passing through. Pray too that the boundary might be elastic, stretching itself to include newcomers, rather than a rigid fence to keep people out.

19 APRIL

If . . .

I say it to my children frequently: 'How would you feel if she did that to you?' I want them to put themselves in someone else's shoes, and appreciate what it would be like to be on the receiving end of their actions. It reminds me of what a powerful word 'If' is:

> It provides for possibility, for miracle . . . 'If' is the imaginative means of projecting somebody else's experiences on to yourself. It is a doorway, leading to empathy, identification, recognition.[13]

In your prayers today, reflect on the power of this little word:

> Lord, Maker of miracles,
> thank you for the spirit of inspiration,
>   invention and discovery
> which makes us wonder,
> 'What would happen if . . .?'
> Inspire me to reshape the world,
> starting with my own life,
> by thinking, 'If things were different . . .'
> Empower me to make change possible
>   by asking if I could make it happen.
> Encourage me to stand in another's shoes
>   by wondering, 'If I were you, how
>   would I feel?'
> and let that empathy change me.
> Amen.

20 APRIL

When?

> For everything there is a season, and a time for every matter under heaven:
>
> a time to be born, and a time to die;
>
> a time to plant, and a time to pluck up what is planted;
>
> a time to kill, and a time to heal;
>
> a time to break down, and a time to build up;
>
> a time to weep, and a time to laugh;
>
> a time to mourn, and a time to dance;
>
> a time to throw away stones, and a time to gather stones together;
>
> a time to embrace, and a time to refrain from embracing;
>
> a time to seek, and a time to lose;
>
> a time to keep, and a time to throw away;
>
> a time to tear, and a time to sew;
>
> a time to keep silence, and a time to speak;
>
> a time to love, and a time to hate;
>
> a time for war, and a time for peace.[14]

In a time of quiet, read and reflect on this well-known passage. Whether you are worried, panicked, oppressed or excited by what the future may hold, let the words speak to you where you are as you bring your concerns to God in prayer.

21 APRIL

But...

It is a risk you always take if you propose a big new idea: you carefully describe your vision, your strategy, your exciting project to those it concerns, and after listening in silence, someone will say, 'But what about...?' It happened to the young P E teacher who proposed a revolutionary new format for Sports Day, and was asked, 'But where are the mums and dads going to sit?' It happened to the vicar who wanted to introduce a new Family Service with tea and cake afterwards, and was asked, 'But what about the mess?'

'But' is so often a negative word, introducing the down side or the nit-picking quibble. It doubts and hesitates, blocks up inspiration, throws obstacles in the path of visionaries and pioneers.

In a time of quiet, bring before God those times when you have felt thwarted by a negative response and perhaps those times when you know you have frustrated others. Pray for the courage and patience to work through those times together.

22 APRIL

... and ...

After a birthday party, my son couldn't tell me fast enough about all the delicious things he had had for tea: 'There was jelly and crisps and little sausages and smiley face biscuits *and* chips *and* lemonade *and* a Scooby Doo birthday cake!'

'And' is a lovely word of addition and inclusion. It reminds me of the way Jesus talked about himself as 'the way, and the truth, and the life',[15] and of the fact that God is Father, Son and Holy Spirit. This is the generous, self-giving God who is not *either* One *or* Three, but *both* himself *and* the Trinity. Perhaps it is no coincidence that our symbol for 'and' is a cross.

In your prayers today, reflect on the abundance of God's gifts, perhaps by listing everything for which you are thankful. Count out your blessings, one after another, and another, and another . . .

23 APRIL

<u>Seeing things differently</u>
Being John Malkovich

A bored filing clerk finds a strange little door in the office one day – and discovers that it leads into the mind of the actor, John Malkovich. Soon he is charging others for the chance to be in someone else's head for fifteen minutes at a time . . .

This extraordinary idea is the premise of the film, *Being John Malkovich*, and it set me thinking: what would I learn if I spent some time in someone else's head? What would they learn in mine that they had never guessed at?

In a time of quiet today, bring before God a person, relationship or situation you are finding difficult. Focus on the problem, then step outwards in prayer, away from yourself, to view it from the other person's perspective. Ask for God's help in making that imaginative leap, and let him speak to you through it.

24 APRIL

Seeing things differently
Seeing the sky

My Canadian friend was the first person I'd met who showed me this country through an outsider's eyes. He used to count the number of days in a row on which we couldn't see the sun for clouds; he was constantly delighted by British politeness and he loved the English countryside. He came from the flat plains of Saskatchewan, a prairie province of Canada, so I could understand why he appreciated our green hills. However, in gaining this beautiful, undulating landscape he had lost something else which I hadn't even considered. He missed the sky. Back home, he could see the sky the way we see it over the sea, stretching wide in all directions until it meets the flat horizon. He could see the weather coming three days away. When he returned home, he would lose our hills and valleys, but he would find that big sky again.

This made me wonder whether the flip side of a loss may sometimes be an unexpected finding. In a time of prayer, turn your losses – whatever they may be – over in your mind, and ask yourself: is there something here for me to find? That finding may not even begin to compensate for the loss, but it may complement it, the loss and the finding together becoming part of your life. Rest in God's presence and hold the lost and the found together in prayer.

25 APRIL

Seeing things differently
Peace talks in the kitchen

There is an ordinary house in Derry, Northern Ireland, in which extraordinary things have happened. It belongs to a man called Brendan Duddy, who for twenty years secretly acted as a go-between for the British government and the IRA. In his own home, he hosted secret talks which played a critical part in bringing about the 1994 cease-fire and thus the Good Friday Agreement. Talking about his role for the first time, he described political discussions of the highest level taking place in an ordinary domestic context. Participants helped clear out the grate and light the fire. While arguing about removal of troops and decommissioning of weapons, they made the tea: 'We want a cease-fire,' alternated with, 'Will you be wanting sugar with that?' There is even a photograph of the president of Sinn Fein in his paisley pyjamas.

> In your prayers today, bring before God
>   all those who work for peace:
> those in presidential palaces and grand
>   embassies, who are engaged in
>   highstakes, high-profile political talks;
> those in safe-houses and anonymous
>   rooms, pursuing secret, risky negotiations;

pray too for those cornered by intractable
conflicts, for those who won't talk and
   won't give an inch of ground;

pray for new light on the problem,
a new way forward, and new hope
for the innocent people who pay
   the price of war.

26 APRIL

Seeing things differently
A glass of water

> 'You'd better be prepared for the jump into hyperspace. It's unpleasantly like being drunk.'
>
> 'What's so unpleasant about being drunk?'
>
> 'You ask a glass of water.'[16]

This conversation is taken from *The Hitchhiker's Guide to the Galaxy*, a book which delights in turning the world as we know it upside down and viewing it from a different angle. The plot hinges on the discovery that the recently demolished Earth was in fact created as a giant computer, and was used in a highly sophisticated experiment run by mice – the same mice that lived in laboratory cages, encouraging humans to believe that we were experimenting on them.

Today, remember that glass of water. In a time of quiet, pray for the grace to see what it is like to be on the receiving end of your actions. Consider how you have behaved towards others; bring your thoughts and feelings, whatever they are, and lay them before God in prayer.

27 APRIL

'Please sit or kneel to pray ...'

When I was taken to church as a child, one of the many things which baffled me was how all the grown-ups knew when to stand, when to sit and so on. In some churches, I still get caught out, and it made me think about our physical positions when we worship and pray.

Standing

> Thousands at his bidding speed
> and post o'er Land and Ocean without rest:
> they also serve, who only stand and wait.[17]

Sometimes it can feel as if others around us are hearing the Lord's call loud and clear: they rush purposefully about doing his work, while we feel like the child in the school play who is fourth spear-bearer, standing on the sidelines feeling rather insignificant.

In a time of quiet, consider that this waiting and watching can be an important way of discovering God's will for us. As a different way of praying, try standing quietly with your hands open before you, waiting to receive.

28 APRIL
Sitting

Sitting down, as far as my grandmother is concerned, is a rare treat: like Martha, run ragged by preparing a meal for Jesus and his friends, she feels that there is always so much to *do*. However, it was Martha's sister Mary who earned Jesus' praise for choosing 'the better part'[18] – sitting at his feet and listening.

Today, reflect on the balance of Martha and Mary in yourself and your life, perhaps using this prayer:

> Lord, I bring before you now
> all the things that I must do today:
> (*name them* . . .)
> Bless my activities, and help me to do my
>   work in your name.
> I offer you this time of sitting still,
>   as Mary did.
> Keep me company in the stillness
> and open my heart and mind to your will.
> Amen.

29 APRIL

Kneeling

> At the name of Jesus
> every knee shall bow,
> every tongue confess him
> King of Glory now.[19]

When we kneel, we acknowledge God's power and authority over us. It is an act of submission and humility: by kneeling we show our dependence on God and our need for mercy and forgiveness.

Today, try kneeling and repeating the words known as the Jesus prayer:

> Lord Jesus Christ, Son of God,
> have mercy on me, a sinner.

Say this over and over again in your prayers, so that saying it becomes automatic. It may seem strange at first, but such repetition is an ancient aid to meditation. Focus on the words, or let your mind float away from them, as you kneel in God's presence.

30 APRIL

Running

> ... let us throw off everything that hinders and the sin that so easily entangles, and let us run with perseverance the race marked out for us.[20]

Paul's powerful image of a runner makes me think of someone struggling with a heavy backpack over bramble-covered scrub land. At last he leaves his pack at a stile and is able to run freely, light-footed and strong, over open fields.

In a time of quiet, reflect on Paul's image and consider what disabilities may be hampering your attempts to run the race which the Lord has marked out for you: fear, lack of confidence, reluctance to get involved, misplaced pride ... In prayer, lay down whatever these burdens may be, asking for forgiveness and strength in Jesus' name.

May

1 MAY
May Day

The May Day holiday has its roots in the celebration of summer's arrival, and also in working-class struggles for justice. In many countries it has been observed as Labour Day since the fight to establish a legally defined working day. In recent years, it has been the focus for anti-capitalist protests, environmental campaigners and political activists of every variety. It has become the day when the people speak out against the global forces which rule their lives.

As a preparation for prayer today, pay attention to the news of this year's May Day protests. Try to suspend your own judgement and look through the banners and stunts to see the stories being told about the state of our world. Remember that 'Mayday' is the international distress signal; what cries for help can you hear? Bring your observations to God in prayer, asking him to speak to you through them. Rest in his presence and listen . . .

2 MAY

Earth

The Cornish town of Padstow is transformed on May Day. The streets and people's hats brim with flowers; every doorway and lamppost is decked with leafy branches, as if the place is bursting with the wealth of our countryside. There are traditional songs and dances and the Obby Oss capers through the streets, as it has done for hundreds of years, bringing in the summer.

Today, make some time to welcome the arrival of summer. Step outside and enjoy this sprouting, greening, blossoming world around us, perhaps using this prayer:

> Creator God,
> Maker of planets and sub-atomic particles,
> Instigator of evolution
> and Champion of wonderful diversity,
> thank you for this rich Earth you have
>   given us.
> Help me to respect its abundant beauty
>   and usefulness;
> show me how to be a careful steward of
>   these natural resources,
> remembering that we have been given this
>   world in trust
> to cherish for future generations.
> Amen.

3 MAY

Water

The charity's advert was deliberately shocking. It aimed to hit home the message that many people in the Third World have no clean drinking water, and that the children are particularly vulnerable to waterborne infections. It showed a chubby, blond toddler making his way alone down the steps to a public toilet beneath a city street. Clutching his beaker, he pottered past the tiled, graffiti-covered walls and towards a cubicle, where he filled his cup from the toilet bowl.

I was reminded of this advert by the approach of Christian Aid Week this month, with its stark slogan, 'We believe in life before death'. So often, the difference between life and death comes down to water. Too little, and there is drought and then famine; too much at once, and there is flooding. Too polluted, and disease is rife.

As a preparation for prayer today, make some time to notice water in all its forms: running in a clean, limitless supply from our taps; pouring rain, grumbled about by one and all; fountains, ponds and garden sprinklers. Remember what it is like to feel really thirsty, or in need of a good wash after doing hot, dusty work. In your prayers, give thanks for the blessing of clean water, and pray for all those whose only source is polluted. Give thanks for an accessible, reliable water supply, and pray for those who have to walk miles to their nearest standpipe or well.

4 MAY

Fire

It was one of the most dazzling things I have ever seen. The Fire Circus exploded into the darkness of the festival field. Fire-jugglers painted arcs of flame on the night and made rings of fire like blazing haloes, while fire-breathers exhaled their dragon's breath. It took me far beyond my cautious fire-lighting and care with matches, reminding me of the thrilling exuberance and playful beauty of fire.

At this time of year, the Church celebrates Pentecost, when the Holy Spirit descended on the disciples and made his power visible in flames above them. In your prayers today, light a candle and reflect on that small, contained fire. Consider it as a tiny representation of the wild, playful, unpredictable blaze that is the Holy Spirit, and pray that you might see those flames burning in the people and the world around you.

5 MAY

Air

> Breathe on me, Breath of God,
> fill me with life anew.[1]

This season of Pentecost is a time to think about the Holy Spirit, or the Holy Ghost. Both terms have a similar root: 'spirit' comes from the Latin word *spiritus*, meaning 'breathing'; 'ghost' comes from the Anglo-Saxon word *gast*, which means 'breath'. The Holy Spirit is the Breath of God, which has the power to breathe new life into us.

Today, make some time to be still and quiet, and simply to breathe. Be aware of your steady breathing, in and out.

As you breathe out, pray: *Breathe on me, Breath of God . . .*

As you breathe in, pray: *Fill me with life anew . . .*

6 MAY

Heat

The scientific evidence is conclusive: our world is getting hotter, and we are beginning to feel the effects. From hurricanes and floods to the food chain disrupted by unseasonal flowering, global warming is proving to be responsible for a lot more than hot weather.

In a time of quiet, consider what you have noticed changing in the world around you. Hold these observations in prayer and bring before God the warming planet he gave us:

> God, our Maker and Master,
> thank you for lending us this Earth.
> It's a bit damaged:
> there's less ice than there was, fewer trees,
> deeper sea and more desert.
> The air has got thicker
> and its outer shell has got thinner –
> and there are a few holes.
> The weather is becoming rather
>   unpredictable.
> And we've lost some of the creatures.
> There's still plenty of us, though –
> more every day.
> Please take this, your blue-green sphere,
> into your healing hands
> and make us whole.
> Amen.

7 MAY

Storm

We were on a camping holiday in Switzerland and the weather was getting hotter and hotter. We pitched our tents that afternoon in a campsite of wide green fields ringed by mountains, then we drove off to find a village where we could have a meal. By the time we had eaten, the air felt sticky and the hazy sky was the colour of an old bruise. It felt like being inside a sealed plastic bag. We drove back towards the mountains and hit a grey wall of rain, beyond which lay our campsite in the shadow of rolling thunderclouds. That night, the storm broke above our heads and rang round the mountains. It was like being inside a giant kettle drum, with each clap of thunder not so much a distant rumble as a terrifying *smack* immediately above us. The next day, the air felt fresh and new, as if it had been scrubbed clean by the storm.

In your prayers today, bring before God those times when you, or those close to you, have been under such intolerable pressure that a storm was bound to break. Name those who are in that position now, perhaps through stress, or debt, or the breakdown of a relationship. Pray that they might weather the storm, and breathe the fresh air of hope and a new beginning.

8 MAY
Wind

There is a wind in southern France which is so overpowering it is called *le Mistral*, meaning 'master'. It has been described as a 'brutal, exhausting wind that can blow the ears off a donkey'[2] and has such a reputation for driving people mad that it has been cited in courts of law as a mitigating factor in cases of violent crime.

In your prayers today, remember all those whose lives are affected by the wind:

> the victims of hurricanes, cyclones and tornadoes;
>
> those without homes who shelter in cardboard boxes, camps or shanty towns;
>
> the fishermen whose livelihood depends on winds and tides;
>
> those living in the desert to whom wind brings choking sand;
>
> those who lose power or communications when the wind blows.

9 MAY

Rain

Rob is a fictional long-distance lorry driver who hates rain. And he drives through a lot of it – so much that he has identified and listed two hundred and thirty-one different kinds of rain.

> And as he drove on, the rainclouds dragged down the sky after him, for, though he did not know it, Rob McKenna was a Rain God. All he knew was that his working days were miserable and he had a succession of lousy holidays. All the clouds knew was that they loved him and wanted to be near him, to cherish him and to water him.[3]

I love the wishful thinking of this science fiction story, which invents a benign, higher purpose behind the apparently random annoyances of life, like drizzle. Sometimes it can seem as if life has got it in for us, and we mutter, 'It never rains but it pours.' A loved one is ill, the washing machine has stopped working, the dog needs to go to the vet and the car has broken down: if you lose your house keys as well that day, it can feel like the end of the world.

In your prayers today, bring before God all those known to you who feel that circumstances are conspiring to make life hard. Pray that they may be given the strength to cope and the hope of a way through.

10 MAY

Cold

> Tonight the temperature will drop even more, and there will be a snowstorm . . . At some point he will stop, and the cold will transform him; like a stalactite, a frozen shell will close around a barely fluid life until even his pulse stops and he becomes one with the landscape. You can't win against the ice.[4]

In your prayers today, remember all those who are fighting against the cold:

> those exposed to the elements by war or disaster;
>
> the survivors and refugees huddled in camps in deserts and mountains, where scorching days turn into freezing nights;
>
> the homeless in our own towns and cities, who rely on blankets, newspapers and cardboard to keep off the frost;
>
> the elderly who cannot afford to heat their homes.

11 MAY
Fog

Living between the Atlantic coast and Bodmin Moor, we get a lot of fog. The last time I got caught in it I was walking the dog in the middle of the afternoon when I suddenly found myself in a thick, white cloud. Sounds were strangely magnified, but I couldn't see where I was, or where the dog was, beyond a couple of feet around me.

It made me think of a medieval book about how to pray, called *The Cloud of Unknowing*. The author believed that to encounter God, you had to ignore all earthly distractions and concentrate only on God. He vividly describes this kind of prayer:

> The first time you do it, you will find nothing but darkness – as it were, a cloud of unknowing. You know nothing, and feel only that your heart and mind are looking God-wards. Whatever you do, this darkness and this cloud is between you and God, preventing you from seeing him clearly by the light of reason ... So stay in this darkness as long as you can, calling out constantly to the God you love; for it may be that if you are ever going to feel him or see him, it will be here, in this cloud and this darkness.[5]

In your prayer time today, try sitting in the dark so that you are not distracted by anything. Simply let the darkness enfold you and let your mind enter 'the cloud of unknowing'. Say, 'Here I am, Lord,' and wait, knowing that – even if you can't see, hear or feel him – he is there with you.

12 MAY
Confused communication

Once upon a time, the Book of Genesis tells us, everyone on earth spoke the same language and managed to co-operate beautifully. They all worked together to build a city with a tower that would reach up to heaven. But God saw what was going on:

> The Lord came down to see the city and the tower, which mortals had built. And the Lord said, 'Look, they are one people, and they have all one language; and this is only the beginning of what they will do; nothing that they propose to do will now be impossible for them. Come, let us go down, and confuse their language there, so that they will not understand one another's speech.' So the Lord scattered them abroad from there over the face of all the earth, and they left off building the city.[6]

This ancient story gives a vivid explanation for the situation we are left with today. In your prayers, bring before God all those who struggle to communicate:

> pray for those who, through illness or disability, find speech hard;
> pray for children trying to make themselves understood;
> for the shy who find it hard to connect;
> for those in broken relationships for whom

every discussion is painful and potentially
 explosive;

for the peacemakers trying to get two
 enemies to talk;

for the asylum-seekers and for all those to
whom our language and our ways are
 strange.

13 MAY

Communicating

It was the day of Pentecost, and the Holy Spirit descended on the disciples:

> All of them were filled with the Holy Spirit and began to speak in other languages, as the Spirit gave them ability. Now there were devout Jews from every nation under heaven living in Jerusalem. And at this sound the crowd gathered and was bewildered, because each one heard them speaking in the native language of each. Amazed and astonished, they asked, 'Are not all these who are speaking Galileans? And how is it that we hear, each of us, in our own native language? . . . – in our own languages we hear them speaking about God's deeds of power.' All were amazed and perplexed, saying to one another, 'What does this mean?' But others sneered and said, 'They are filled with new wine.'[7]

Filled with the Holy Spirit, the first act of the embryonic Christian Church was to speak out to a great crowd of people from all over the world, and to communicate in a way which each of them could understand. It was an act of outreach and inclusion, sensitive to the needs of individuals (they spoke in *everyone's* native language), dismissed by some ('They must be drunk!') yet embracing all.

Whatever your experience of church, in your prayers today reflect on its inspiration. Rest in God's presence and share with him your feelings about church in the light of the fire of Pentecost.

14 MAY
Translating

In the small, Irish-speaking community of Baile Beag, some British soldiers have arrived. It is 1833 and their job is to make a new map of the country. This involves translating and 'standardising' every single place-name from Gaelic into English, for example so that *Bun na hAbhann*, which means 'the end of the river', becomes Burnfoot. The young officer who attempts this task becomes attached to the land he is trying to translate, and grows increasingly concerned about the work he has been ordered to do. He says, 'It's an eviction of sorts . . . Something is being eroded.'[8]

The events of this modern play raise some interesting questions about language, homeland and identity. In a time of quiet, bring before God all those who feel lost in translation:

> pray for those who are trying to hold on
> to their language before it is squeezed out
>   of existence –
>
> for those who speak Welsh, Gaelic,
>   Cornish and other minority languages;
>
> pray for the refugees who are uprooted
>   from their native land and language;
>
> for the immigrant families who want to
>   start a new life;
>
> for their children, speaking one language
>   at home and another at school,

and for all those who think and feel in
one language whilst struggling to express
themselves in another.

15 MAY

Interpreting

> . . . Jesus knelt to share with thee
> the silence of eternity,
> interpreted by love.[9]

In your prayers today, consider your own experience of silence, perhaps using these words:

> Loving Lord,
> in the love I share with others,
> I thank you that my words,
> unspoken and misspoken,
> the thoughts which I mangle in sentences
> and the feelings which struggle to find a voice
> are interpreted and understood by love.
> In your love for me,
> I thank you that when I am lost for words,
> when pain has made me dumb
> or stubbornness has shut my mouth
>   and mind,
> when I cannot or will not pray,
> my silence is interpreted and understood
>   by love.
> Amen.

16 MAY
Code

At a party in the White House, the secretary to the Chief of Staff, Leo McGarry, politely interrupts a conversation. She addresses a man with the words, 'Leo McGarry would like you to meet an old friend of his.'[10] The man makes his excuses and leaves the room with her immediately, because the innocuous phrase is a White House code which means, 'Something serious has happened. You are needed in the Situation Room right now.'

This moment from the TV drama, *The West Wing*, reminds me that there are times when we speak in code, even though every word can be understood by our listeners. In a time of quiet, reflect on those times when you do not say what you mean, for example when you have said, 'No, really, I'm fine,' and meant, 'I really need some help.' Recall those times when you have taken someone else's words at face value, and taken them amiss, or misunderstood the real message. Pray for the wisdom to see when an angry word or a cold rebuff is a cry for help, and to understand how best to respond.

17 MAY

Breaking the code

Alan Turing was a mathematician who was instrumental in breaking the Enigma code used by the Germans in the Second World War. The play which dramatises his life has a punning title, *Breaking the Code*[11]: it refers both to his work on Enigma and to his hidden homosexuality. His story is one of isolation and despair as he found himself unable to conform to the social norms of his time.

In your prayers today, pray for all those who break the codes of our modern times:

> the socially excluded, who can't find work and can't make ends meet;
>
> the stigmatised youths in hooded tops;
>
> the marginalised travellers;
>
> the unwanted homeless;
>
> those in positions of authority who won't toe the party line;
>
> those who question the might of market forces;
>
> those who tell inconvenient truths,
>
> and all those known to you who feel at odds with the world.

18 MAY

Scattered bones

The prophet Ezekiel is taken by the Lord to a valley full of dry bones. He is called to tell these piles of bones that the Lord is going to make them live again:

> Suddenly there was a noise, a rattling, and the bones came together, bone to its bone. I looked, and there were sinews on them, and flesh had come upon them, and skin had covered them; but there was no breath in them. Then he said to me, 'Prophesy to the breath, prophesy, mortal, and say to the breath: Thus says the Lord God: Come from the four winds, O breath, and breathe upon these slain, that they may live.' I prophesied as he commanded me, and the breath came into them, and they lived, and stood on their feet, a vast multitude.[12]

This scene is a powerful vision of rebirth. These people were not just dead – their bones had been picked clean by the desert birds and were left scattered. This was the fate of exiles and defeated warriors: their bodies were left to become anonymous bones, cast out and forgotten. From this outer darkness of disgrace, and from physical dismemberment and decay, God calls and revives a multitude of people.

continued overleaf

In a time of quiet, bring before God all those who feel fractured, broken apart, dried up or discarded. Pray for those you know, and those you don't know; hold them in your prayers, saying:

> Breath of God, breathe upon them,
> so that they might live.

19 MAY

Mending brokenness

> Batter my heart, three-personed God;
>   for, you
> as yet but knock, breathe, shine, and seek
>   to mend;
> that I may rise, and stand, o'erthrow me,
>   and bend
> your force, to break, blow, burn, and
>   make me new.[13]

Breathe, shine, and seek to mend

This poem describes two ways in which God's power can change lives. First, there is the gentle approach: God seeks to mend our brokenness by bathing us in the radiance of his love and breathing his life-giving Spirit upon us.

In your prayers, bring to mind your experience of such transformation, in your own life or those close to you:

> give thanks for a spirit which feels revived;
> for the relief of mental or physical suffering;
> for the sense of calm which soothes those who were afraid;
> for the refreshment of those who were overburdened;
> for comfort experienced by those who grieve;
> for peace felt by those who had struggled to find rest.

20 MAY

Batter my heart . . . and make me new

The poet, however, feels parts of him are so resistant to change that they need to be spiritually battered and beaten into submission. His life is like a badly mended bone, misshapen and painful, which needs to be broken and re-set to be made good and whole again.

Today, pray for those people, places and situations which are in need of such radical healing, such tough divine love:

> intractable conflicts throughout the world;
>
> relationships throttled by anger and pain;
>
> individuals and their families imprisoned by addiction or violence;
>
> the darkest parts of ourselves which we refuse to examine in the sight of God.

For each prayer intention, try using this as your bidding:

> Father, bend your force to break and make us new.

21 MAY

Broken things

> You can have my heart
> if you don't mind broken things.[14]

The words of this love song can also be read as a humble offering of ourselves to God. We are broken people, and sometimes we are not much to be proud of, yet still God loves us and calls us to him.

In your prayers, confess those things in your life that are broken, and have perhaps been so for many years. Admit to your flaws and failings, and lay all the broken pieces in the hands of the loving God who wants to make you whole again.

22 MAY

Picking up the pieces

I have a friend whose talent is ceramic art. She had not made anything for several years until, in her walks along the beaches near her home, she started picking up pieces of pottery, china and worn glass. She used these to make exquisite mosaic bowls, finding a special grace and a real spiritual fulfilment in gathering up what was broken and making it into something beautiful and new.

In your prayers today, reflect on your own life, and the network of lives and relationships of which you are part; pray for eyes to see what is broken, and a heart to sense how it might be made whole. Reflect that Christ has no hands on earth to heal, but ours . . .

23 MAY
Patchwork

When I was little, my mum made patchwork quilts for the whole family. The patchwork was made of simple squares, but it was true patchwork, created in the spirit of 'make do and mend' from pieces of worn-out clothes and scraps of leftover material. These quilts are still in one piece, and my sister and I can look at them and remember the favourite dresses and old bedroom curtains from which ours were made.

I think of my spiritual journey as patchwork: it is not especially beautiful, and some bits of it are tatty while other bits are new. It is a work in progress, made by me and of me, with bits of memory and experience layered one on top of the other. But all these odds and ends are also subject to God's transforming power, and he can change and remake the patchwork if I let him in.

In a time of quiet, consider the bits and pieces that make up your own spiritual life. Offer them to God in prayer, waiting to see what you and he might make of them together.

24 MAY
Song of joy

They had run away from the slave-quarters in Egypt, with the wailing of bereaved Egyptian mothers ringing in their ears. They escaped into the desert with small children, animals and whatever belongings they could carry, guided by miraculous columns of cloud and fire. Then Pharoah's army comes after them, mounted on chariots, every officer driven by grief and rage at the loss of his eldest child. Hounded to the edge of the Red Sea, the people are close to despair – until God tells Moses to part the water before them. A fierce wind blasts the waves apart and clears a sandy path for the Israelites, who walk across the sea bed between two roaring, towering walls of water, having to trust that the miracle will hold until they are all on the other side. They make it – but the Egyptians are still following them. At that moment, God tells Moses to close the waters and the sea returns, drowning the entire army.[15]

What would those left on the shore be feeling? Shock and awe, certainly, but the overwhelming feelings are relief and sheer joy: they are safe. The first thing they do is sing.

Today, find a piece of music which, for you, expresses a feeling of pure joy. Play it yourself or listen to it as loud as possible, and lose yourself in the feelings of delight it gives you. Let your prayer of joy and thankfulness well up through the music.

25 MAY

The singing bowl

It looks rather like a large pestle and mortar: it is a round, metal bowl with a suede-covered wooden cylinder sitting inside. It would take you a while to work out what it was for if no one showed you. What this bowl does, in an eerily beautiful way, is sing. You rub the suede beater slowly and firmly around the rim, just as you might rub a wet finger around the top of a wineglass. In the same way, if you do it right, a ringing note begins to sound. With the singing bowl, it can start as a quiet hum and swell to a full, bell-like sound which seems to well up out of the bowl.

These bowls originated in the east, where they have long been used by Buddhists as a tool for meditation and prayer. In a time of quiet today, try using a wine glass as your own singing bowl, or simply sit with an empty bowl in your hands and stir up the sound in your imagination. Don't worry about what to pray: let your prayer grow out of the repetitive action and the sound, then slowly let both dwindle into silence and stillness.

26 MAY

Songlines

The Aboriginal people of Australia have an ancient way of understanding their landscape and identity. For them, in the beginning there was the Dreamtime, and their ancestors created themselves as all the different species and spread across the country, each leaving behind him 'a trail of words and musical notes' known as a Dreaming-track or Songline. These Songlines became a way for Aboriginals to identify with their particular ancestor, to read his story in the features of the landscape and to navigate across the country. The Songline was also a line of communication, connecting people who shared the same ancestor and binding them as brothers and sisters.[16]

We may not sing it, but we all have our own ways of connecting ourselves to the world we inhabit. My children do it by naming things: by the river where we often walk our dog, they have christened Dragonfly Corner and Heron's Pool; further up the hill is the Bonkers Field, so called because of the dog's wild enjoyment of the long grass which grows there. In your prayers today, bring before God your own relationship to the landscape around you, and the favourite places which you feel belong to you. Pray for his blessing on them, and pray that through them, he might speak to you about his creation.

27 MAY

Rooted in music

> Without our stories or our songs
> how will we know where we come from?[17]

These lines come from a modern song which makes an impassioned plea for the survival of English folk songs. The writers envy the Celt, with his ballads and ceilidhs, and they pity the young people of England, brought up on a diet of American music and culture, for whom expressing their Englishness in song means 'Swing low, sweet chariot', at the rugby. Traditional English songs are being lost, and with them a part of our national identity.

In a time of quiet, reflect on the songs which remind you where you come from: the nursery rhymes, playground songs, football chants, school hymns and music you listened to as you were growing up. Sing or play some of it today, and give thanks for that sense of your roots and identity which the music gives you.

28 MAY

Singing

In the bath or in the shower, we can be the singers we wish we were. Relaxed, uninhibited and (hopefully) unheard, we can breathe deeply and sing out. Songs of joy, passion or longing reverberate in our private acoustic chamber.

There is a long tradition of sung prayers in the Christian church, from monastic plainsong to Taizé chants and modern worship choruses. Whatever kind of voice you have, there is something powerful about letting a prayer fly in song, like unspooling a string as a kite takes off.

In your prayers today, sing something simple. It may be a chant or a line from a hymn that you know, or it could be a simple phrase, repeated on a single note, perhaps growing louder and then softer with each repetition:

> sing, 'Holy, holy, holy Lord,'
> or, 'Lord, have mercy,
> Christ have mercy.'

Trusting that God is listening, let your prayer unwind and fly in song.

29 MAY
Humming

> The more it snows
>   (tiddely pom),
> the more it goes
>   (tiddely pom),
> the more it goes
>   (tiddely pom),
> on snowing.[18]

In eastern religions there is a repetitive form of prayer based on the 'mantra', which is a sacred word or phrase, sung or spoken repeatedly as a meditation. I was delighted recently to read about an English man who often prays in this way and thinks of his mantra as a 'hum',[19] recalling the rhymes Winnie-the-Pooh composed while walking. To me, the idea of using a 'hum' in prayer seems more familiar and understandable.

For your prayers today, make time to go for a walk. Relax into the rhythm of walking and let a prayerful 'hum' come from inside you, or inwardly repeat a phrase which keeps time with your footsteps, for example: 'Lord, have mercy,' 'Christ be with me,' or, 'Bless this walking.' Let your prayer grow out of the repetition, or let it be the repetition itself.

30 MAY

Drumming

In the middle of Carnival Day, the main square of our small town was given over to a drumming display. There were about twenty drummers: shirtless young men with green hair and piercings stood at the back with drums which came up nearly to their waists; grandmothers sat on the floor with round, hide-covered drums which they beat with their palms; young women and teenagers played drums which hung from their shoulders or held bodhrums, their hands working in a fluttering motion. The sound was powerful and hypnotic – I didn't so much hear it as feel it, because the air was throbbing and the ground vibrating through the soles of my feet.

In a time of quiet today, try drumming up prayer. Find something on which you can beat out a rhythm, even if it is a table-top or simply your hands. It may seem strange at first, but start to drum, letting the rhythmic patterns take over. When you feel surrounded by the sound, begin to slow it down and soften it until you are resting in silence. Offer that quiet space to God and open your mind in prayer.

31 MAY

Sound of silence

One of the most unusual musical compositions of recent times is John Cage's piece entitled *4' 33"*. When it is performed, the pianist sits down, with a stopwatch, and plays absolutely nothing for exactly four minutes and thirty-three seconds. The piece consists of silence and whatever background noises happen to be audible during the performance.

Today, set aside a fixed period of time in which to be completely silent and still, as if you were an audience member listening intently to that deliberate silence. Notice the sounds which creep into the quietness, or simply rest. Offer that silence to God, to do with as he will.

June

1 JUNE

Learning

> She has a gift to teach, a sacred gift. Fifteen years in dreary bluish-green classrooms, pacing as she talks, this solid woman carries a flame. She cares what she says, if it is precisely truthful and if it can be heard correctly; her dark eyes flash, her hands flutter, she lifts her head and stands on tiptoe to give the sentence coming out of her mouth a little more arc.[1]

In a time of quiet, bring to mind your school days and remember an inspiring teacher. Recollect what you were like at that age, and what you learned from that person; remember what it was about them that inspired you then, and has stayed with you ever since. Thank God for that great gift, cherishing it in prayer.

2 JUNE

Revision

When I was at school and facing the onset of exams, I used to feel like a reluctant competitor at an eating contest: I was overwhelmed and somewhat sickened by the mountain of knowledge in front of me that I was required to ingest in a short period of time. I kept those feelings at bay by creating beautiful, hand-drawn revision timetables, with every subject colour-coded in different highlighter pens. I could spend hours making a timetable, giving myself almost the same sense of achievement as would have been produced by actually doing some revision.

In your prayers today, bring before God any big, unpleasant task which is looming over you. Lay down before him your feelings of fear, anxiety, stress and reluctance. Confess your own tendency to distract and divert yourself from the task, whatever it may be, and pray for the will to begin it and the strength to complete it.

3 JUNE

Testing

8. Have you the faintest recollection of
   a) Ethelbreth?
   b) Athelthral?
   c) Thruthelthrolth?

9. What have you the faintest recollection of?

   ... N.B. Do not attempt to answer more than one question at a time.[2]

This spoof history examination reads like a pre-exam nightmare of impossible questions. In your prayers today, remember all those who are feeling tested at this time:

> students who are taking their exams;
>
> teachers who feel their own skills are under scrutiny;
>
> those involved in sporting competitions;
>
> and all those who fear that months and years of hard work may count for nothing;
>
> pray also for those known to you whose endurance is being tested by difficult times.

4 JUNE
Results

I had the letter in my hand. I had been badgering the postman for it for days and it was here at last. I held it, boggling at that slim envelope's potential to change my life. I couldn't decide whether to open it in front of my family or in private. I raced up to my room and shut the bedroom door. I had to do it: I tore it open and scanned the page just long enough to discover that it was good news, it was everything I'd hoped for. Then I burst out of my room to tell everyone, smacking the door open with such force that I broke the handle against the wall.

That moment before you know the result is charged with fierce anticipation and dread. In your prayers, remember all those who face their results today:

> those receiving a diagnosis;
>
> those awaiting a judgement in court;
>
> those facing an investigation or tribunal;
>
> those preparing for a job interview;
>
> those anticipating exam results;
>
> pray for all those bracing themselves for the worst while longing for the best.

5 JUNE

Sensory prayer
Sight

The monks who illuminated the medieval Gospel manuscripts understood the 'beauty of holiness'.[3] They made their sacred texts into works of art, with jewels on the cover and gold leaf flashing on every intricate, highly coloured page. These books were their life's work, and their life's prayer – an act of artistic and spiritual devotion.

Today, try praying an active form of prayer by making something beautiful. This could be a painting, a piece of woodwork, a flowerbed or a beautifully laid table for a cherished guest. Whatever you do, do it prayerfully, in Jesus' name.

6 JUNE

Sensory prayer
Sound

Noise pollution is a fact of modern life. Against a background of traffic noise and the quiet hum of electrical equipment on standby, there are all the beeps, buzzes and annoying ring-tones of our indispensable gadgets.

Today, try to leave behind all the distractions and find a place in which to be quiet. Set aside some time simply to rest in the silence. At the end of that time, settle down to really *listen* to something beautiful: a piece of music, evening birdsong, a running stream – whatever it is, give it your full attention. Pray that you might practise this profoundly attentive listening in other situations: in conversations with others and when you are offering up a time of silence to God.

7 JUNE

Sensory prayer
Smell

Beautiful smells have an ancient association with holiness. Incense is used in many religions and in many Christian churches as a sign of prayers being offered to God; Christ was presented with frankincense and myrrh at his birth, and later his feet were anointed with spikenard, a fabulously exotic perfume.

In a time of quiet, find the most beautiful smell you can: burn some essential oils or a scented candle, have a posy of sweet peas by your side or open the window to the smell of freshly cut grass. Let the fragrance fill up your senses as you rest in God's presence. Thank God for the beauty of it, and in prayer open your mind and heart to his grace.

8 JUNE

Sensory prayer
Touch

A traditional Anglican church is not a place of exuberant physical contact. Members of the congregation sit at a socially acceptable distance from one another, and even when touching is required – during the Sharing of the Peace – it is generally done at arm's length, with a handshake. Yet originally the Peace was a kiss, shared by members of the second-century church as a sign of the bonds of love and peace which held them together as a community.

In your prayers today, consider the importance of touch:

> Father God,
> thank you for the human touch:
> the embrace of love or comfort,
> the handshake which offers a welcome
> or seals a peace treaty,
> the reassuring hand on the shoulder,
> the cuddles and hugs with our small children.
>
> Brother Christ,
> you reached out throughout your life
> to touch the untouchables.
> May we, who are your hands on earth,
> follow your example when we encounter those
>   whom our society rejects.

continued overleaf

Go-Between Spirit,
in our relationships with others
help us to know when a human touch
  is needed,
and inspire us to reach out and make contact.
Amen.

9 JUNE

Sensory prayer
Taste

For the French writer, Marcel Proust, the thing that triggered memories of his past most strongly was a little buttery cake, the madeleine. My husband relives his childhood every time he treats himself to a quarter of old-fashioned sweets: one taste of a butterscotch pillow or a sherbet fountain and he's a happy seven-year-old again.

Taste has a powerful connection with memory. As a preparation for prayer, taste something which brings back memories for you, or recall that taste as strongly as you can. Let the memories flood in and hold them in prayer, thanking God for them, whatever they may be.

10 JUNE
A curse

The two Roman noblewomen were deadly enemies. Atia had imprisoned and tortured Servilia, who then returned to curse her. Servilia, dressed in sackcloth and grey with ashes, sat outside Atia's door and shouted over and over, 'Atia of the Julii, I call for justice!' She continued day and night until Atia, nearly driven mad by the constant calling, went outside to confront her accuser. Looking her enemy straight in the eye, Servilia called upon the gods to curse her: 'Send her bitterness and despair for all of her life.' Servilia then killed herself to seal the curse with her own blood.

This scene, from the TV drama *Rome*,[4] showed the power of a Roman curse, and I was struck by the fact that it began with a call for justice. I recently encountered curses in a Christian context which were inspired by a longing for social and political justice. They began, 'Cursed be . . . ' and condemned such things as the persecution of children and the pollution of our world.[5]

In your prayers today, try making a list of those things which you hate and deplore. Introduce each item with the words, 'Cursed be . . .'. When you have exhausted your list, offer it to God in prayer and rest in his presence, listening to him through the ringing echo of your curses.

11 JUNE

Cursed

There is a devastating little service tucked away in *The Book of Common Prayer* which is called, 'A Commination or denouncing of God's anger and judgements against sinners'. It is written for use at the beginning of Lent, to encourage penitence by reminding the congregation of God's condemnation of sin. It is a litany of curses, each one of which is confirmed by the people:

> Minister: Cursed are the unmerciful, fornicators, and adulterers, covetous persons, idolaters, slanderers, drunkards, and extortioners.
>
> Answer: Amen.[6]

In a time of quiet, call to mind those things for which you need forgiveness: the thoughts, the words spoken, the things done and not done. Cast them away from yourself with a curse; disown them and accept instead God's offer of forgiveness and a clean slate.

12 JUNE

Blessing in disguise

In the story of the Sleeping Beauty, the trouble starts with a curse. All the good fairies who have attended the baby princess' christening have showered their blessings upon her, but the bad fairy who was not invited curses her, saying that she will prick her finger on the spindle of a spinning wheel on her sixteenth birthday, and she will die. The curse cannot be undone, but the last fairy to give her blessing softens it, and changes death to a hundred-year-long sleep. The curse is fulfilled, but I have always wondered whether it was, in fact, a blessing in disguise. The young princess falls asleep on the threshold of adulthood, and her hundred years of suspended animation end with true love's kiss and her wedding. The curse has enabled her to leapfrog all the trial and error, hope, heartbreak and confusion which normally mark those coming-of-age years.

In your prayers today, remember all those children who are turning into adults:

> pray for those coming to terms with a grown-up world;
> for those struggling with new responsibilities;
> for those trying to understand their sexuality;
> for those trying to build relationships;
> for those revelling in their independence;

for those challenged by their studies;
for those who have left school;
for those who have lost all direction
and for those who are trying to find
 themselves.

13 JUNE

A mixed blessing

There is a famous old cartoon which shows a nervous curate dining with a bishop. Peering at the young man's plate, the bishop exclaims, 'I'm afraid you've got a bad egg, Mr Jones!'

Eager to please, the curate replies, 'Oh no, my Lord, I assure you! Parts of it are excellent!'[7]

This has given us the phrase, 'a bit of a curate's egg', which has come to mean 'a mixture of good and bad parts'.

In a time of quiet, reflect on those parts of your life which may best be described as a mixed blessing. Hold in prayer those things about which it is hard to be wholly thankful; recognise the goodness as well as the pain or problems, and let God speak to you through both.

14 JUNE
Counting blessings

The arrival of the cricket season reminds me of a nugget of information my brain has retained from childhood: umpires count the number of balls in an over by using pebbles, marbles or coins. They keep six in one pocket, and as each ball is bowled they transfer one to the other pocket.

This idea of physical counting appeals to me, because it is felt rather than thought. As a preparation for prayer today, collect a pile of small stones or pebbles. In a time of quiet, call to mind all those things with which your life has been blessed. Thank God for each one and as you do so, put one stone on top of another, until you have a heap or tower (known as a 'cairn') of blessing-stones in front of you. Keep it and add to it, as a physical reminder of how much you have been given.

15 JUNE

Blessed

There are blessings for journeys:

> May the road rise to meet you,
> may the wind be always at your back,
> may the sun shine warm upon your face,
> the rains fall soft upon your fields and,
> until we meet again,
> may God hold you in the palm of
>   his hand.[8]

There are blessings for the home:

> Lord, bless this house with [*the names of the people*] who make it their home. Defend it with your heavenly grace, and create within its walls a place of warmth, love and safety.[9]

I have found blessings for vehicles, workplaces, rings, flags and musical instruments. There is, it seems, nothing in our lives which cannot be offered to God for his blessing.

In your prayers today, offer something of yours for God's blessing. Try using the words, 'Blessed be . . .' or, 'Peace be upon . . .' and name it. Make a list, and create a litany of blessings.

16 JUNE

Deep peace of the running wave to you[10]

Standing on a North Cornish beach, I watch the Atlantic rollers smashing on to the rocks and wonder where deep peace is to be found in these waves. Nevertheless, after a while, the repetitive rhythm of the rising and breaking surf is strangely calming. Perhaps this is not so surprising. Repetition has always had a place in the spiritual life: think of the Roman Catholic counting Hail Marys on her rosary beads or the Hindu repeating his mantra. Psychologists believe that such repetition can open up deeper levels of consciousness and lead to a more profound prayerful state.

In your prayer time, try using repetition to lead you to a deeper peace. Taizé chants are a good way to start, spoken or sung if you know the tunes:

> Bless the Lord, my soul,
> and bless God's holy name.
> Bless the Lord, my soul,
> who leads me into life.

> Jesus, remember me
> when you come into your kingdom.
> Jesus, remember me
> when you come into your kingdom.[11]

Use the repetition to occupy the busy, everyday part of your brain that is so easily distracted; relax and let the deeper part of your mind open in prayer.

17 JUNE

Deep peace of the flowing air to you

I had not understood, before we moved close to the Atlantic coast, how our lives would be dominated by the weather, and especially the wind. The movement of weather fronts dictates how long we can expect to spend on the beach; too much or too little wind affects our plans to go sailing. Other mums in the playground all wear hats or hooded coats, and after my hair has been wrapped round my face by the wind a few times, I understand why. The wind turbines spin on the headland. I even met a local man selling reclaimed wooden furniture who only opens his workshop when the wind is in the right direction because, 'Those south-westerlys blow the damp straight in the door.'

This quirk of Cornish life reminds me that wind has long been used as a metaphor to help us understand the mystery of the Holy Spirit. The words for Spirit, in the languages of the Bible (*ruach* in Hebrew, *pneuma* in Greek, *spiritus* in Latin), all mean 'wind' or 'breath'.[12] This driving force of life, which can break down trees, fill a sail or gently ruffle our hair, is the same substance as the breath of life. It is at work in the world and an intimate part of our living, breathing bodies. For your prayers today, get out into the fresh air and breathe deeply. Reflect on the Spirit of God which, like the wind, is flowing all around you and inside you at the same time, and open your heart to his power.

18 JUNE

Deep peace of the quiet earth to you

We live on the edge of Bodmin Moor, and if I need some peace I head for Roughtor, the second highest point on the moor and a place of stark, wild beauty. Green moorland spreads out and leads upwards, gently at first, to a rugged summit which seems to be made entirely of granite boulders and huge cairns. As you wander the slopes among wild ponies and sheep, clambering over the remains of ancient stone huts, what settles on you is the deep silence of the moor. There are no people or roads within earshot, no trees or bushes to whistle in the wind, just the tough, cropped grass and the stones. It's quiet enough to hear tiny chirrups of distant birdsong and the buzz of passing insects; it's so quiet, a sheep's bleat can make you jump.

As part of your prayers, leave behind the busyness of work and home, and head for the hills – or the fields, woods, river or coast – in search of your own peaceful place. Open your mind and heart to the deep peace of the quiet earth, remembering the words of Psalm 23:

> The Lord is my shepherd, I shall not want.
> He makes me lie down in green pastures;
> he leads me beside still waters;
> he restores my soul.[13]

19 JUNE

Deep peace of the shining stars to you

At the beginning of the film, *A Matter of Life and Death*, an airman in the Second World War is about to jump from his burning plane high above the Atlantic. But, as he puts it, there's a catch: no parachute. He's going to die. However, this intensely dramatic moment is not where the film starts. The first thing we see is a long, beautiful tracking shot of outer space. Galaxies shimmer and planets spin and gleam, while the voice-over comments, 'This is space. Big, isn't it?' Gradually the camera moves us closer to our own solar system until we can identify a familiar blue-green planet; nearer still and we can see continents and weather systems – 'Looks like fog over the Atlantic.' Only when we are taken into the fog do we meet the airman in his stricken plane, and this extraordinary story of heaven and earth, life and death begins.[14]

It's a powerful piece of cinema which plays on that sense we all recognise when gazing into the dizzying depth of a starry night: a feeling that the stars, so ancient and so incredibly distant, put our troubled lives into perspective. As part of your prayers, seek this new perspective. Perhaps you could sit quietly and contemplate the stars one night, or you could view the earth from space via the Internet. Look up Google Earth and watch in wonder as you move through space to find your own continent, country, town and street. Watch – and listen to God.

20 JUNE

Deep peace of the Son of Peace to you

> O God, from whom all holy desires, all good counsels, and all just works do proceed: Give unto thy servants that peace which the world cannot give . . .[15]

When I was a stressed and anxious undergraduate, these words in College Evensong used to leap out at me. No matter how much I tried to find some peace through my friendships, my studies or my enjoyment of the natural world, I would never find that deep peace I longed for unless I let God in.

The need for that peace which the world cannot give is one of our deepest, most universal desires: it finds expression in the Hebrew greeting, *Shalom*, in Muslim reverence for the prophet Muhammad – 'Peace be upon him' – and in countless Christian benedictions. Anglican churchgoers are dismissed with the blessing that begins:

> The peace of God, which passes all understanding, keep your hearts and minds in the knowledge and love of God . . .[16]

In a time of quiet, simply rest, breathing deeply and steadily. Call to mind those known to you who need that peace which the world cannot give, and pray for the deep peace of the Son of Peace.

21 JUNE
Finding the truth

Some years ago, Paulina was raped and tortured at the hands of an oppressive regime, possibly in Chile. She never saw her attackers, or the doctor from whom they took orders. On this particular night, her husband returns home with a stranger who helped him when his car broke down. The man is a doctor, and Paulina becomes increasingly convinced that he is the man who oversaw her rape and torture. In this intense play,[17] the audience is often unsure of the truth: is the doctor really the torturer? Is Paulina rationally convinced or is her belief the product of her trauma and paranoia? After she holds him at gunpoint and forces a confession from him, does she kill him or let him go? We never know for sure.

In your prayers today, bring before God all those who are trying to find out the truth in the messy aftermath of violence, war or an overthrown dictatorship. Pray for all those seeking justice, truth and reconciliation – and pray too for those who only crave revenge.

22 JUNE
Seeing the truth

> She read it every day . . . and she found that she could sink more and more readily into the calm state in which the symbol-meanings clarified themselves, and those great mountain-ranges touched by sunlight emerged into vision.[18]

This description comes from Philip Pullman's *Northern Lights*. Its heroine, Lyra, is skilled at deception, yet she has been given a mysterious and powerful object called an alethiometer. It is a truth-teller which looks rather like a compass and combines symbols in complex combinations to reveal its meaning. The way Lyra reads it is strikingly prayerful: she sinks into this meditative state and feels for meaning 'like climbing down a ladder at night'. This involves a different way of seeing, '. . . like focusing your eyes'.[19]

In a time of quiet, call to mind anything which is complicated and confusing in your life at the moment. Bring the whole tangled mess, whatever it is, to God in prayer, and rest in his presence. Don't try to find a way through it; simply let your mind relax and sink into the problem, trusting in his power to make things clear.

23 JUNE

Secrets and lies

The climactic scene of the film *Secrets and Lies* is an explosion of revelations and their emotional repercussions. A mother's secretly adopted daughter, a wife's secret battle against infertility, hidden pain and resentment – everything is brought out in the open. The effect is devastating, but ultimately it proves to have opened a door for all those family members who had been trapped by their deceptions. The closing scenes of the film point to a more hopeful future.

In your prayers today, bring before God all those affected by secrets and lies:

> the spouse who has just discovered an affair;
> the child who has found out who Daddy really is;
> the victims who have concealed their abuse;
> the addicts who admit to their addiction,
> and all those who have hidden the truth from those closest to them, through fear, shame or denial.

Hold them together in prayer:

> Lord, you are the Truth;
> heal those hurt by hard truths
> and damaged by lies.
> Show them your Way
> and bring them to new life in you.
> Amen.

24 JUNE
Home truths

Sometimes the truth really does hurt. It can hurt to hear it, and hurt to tell it, because it demands a painful nakedness. To tell the truth we have to strip off all those little fibs and flimsy pretences which have covered us up, and bare all. It reminds me of C. S. Lewis' description of the 'real nakedness of the soul in prayer'[20]: being honest to God requires that same kind of exposure.

In a time of prayer, admit to yourself and to God all those ways in which you have failed to tell the truth to him, to others and to yourself. Expose it all in prayer, and if it helps, pray while naked as a reminder of how that makes you feel – awkward and vulnerable, perhaps, but also unencumbered, even liberated. Remember Jesus' words: 'The truth will make you free.'[21]

25 JUNE

Hidden truths

At the time I am writing this, police are uncovering the secrets of the former children's home at Haut de la Garenne in Jersey. They have unearthed the blocked-up cellars which may have been the 'punishment rooms' in which abuse took place. Investigators have found fragments of bone and children's teeth, and some chilling graffiti on the underground walls: someone had written, 'I've been bad for years and years.'

In your prayers today, remember all those who are affected whenever truth is kept hidden:

> pray for the victims, who long for
>   justice and peace of mind;
> pray for the failed whistle-blowers, who
>   suspected but did nothing;
> pray for the perpetrators whom no one
>   wants to pray for;
> pray for the families of the 'disappeared'
>   throughout the world,
> left knowing nothing but fearing the worst;
> pray for all those whose loved ones are
> missing, who just want to find out what
>   happened;
> pray for those known to you
> and those known only to God
> who are hiding the truth, even from
>   themselves.

26 JUNE

Hidden in plain sight

At the end of the film, *The Thomas Crown Affair*, the hero is in New York's Metropolitan Museum of Art with a stolen painting. He is wearing a bowler hat and carrying a briefcase. He looks so distinctive that the plainclothes policemen and security guards who are waiting to catch him are sure he will not escape this time. However, at the critical moment, the crowded staircases and halls of the museum fill with men in bowler hats who are carrying briefcases. They move in all directions, pursued by various guards, and in the confusion Thomas Crown slips away.

I love the ingenuity of this trick, which relies on being noticed and remaining in plain sight in order to hide. It made me wonder whether things are hidden from us in this way in our everyday lives. In your prayers today, rest in God's presence and ask him to open your eyes to see the truth of the people and the world around you. Be attentive, and ask: what is so obvious that I have failed to notice it?

27 JUNE

Weddings
Old

We are deep in wedding season now, and the prayers for the next four days have been suggested by that wedding day maxim, 'Something old, something new, something borrowed, something blue.'

> Have mercy on us, O Lord, have mercy on us, and let us both grow old together in health.[22]

This prayer is from a marriage blessing, and I was struck by its focus on old age. It reminds me of the big wedding anniversaries: forty years of marriage is the ruby wedding; fifty is golden and sixty is diamond. These names suggest that, in spite of all the fanfare surrounding a young couple on their wedding day, marriage gets more precious as the years go by.

In your prayers today, bring before God all those long marriages known to you. Give thanks for lasting love which is deep and strong and has endured many things. Give thanks for the blessing of a lifelong commitment, and for the comfort of a shared journey.

28 JUNE

Weddings
New

> I was like a species that hadn't even realised it lived in a near-desert till one day its taproot hit water. Now I had taken a whole new shape. No, I had taken the shape I was always supposed to, the shape that let me hold my head high.[23]

I was touched by this vivid description of the transforming, life-giving power of love. In your prayers today, reflect on the feeling of finding true love, as you have experienced it yourself or seen it in those close to you. Give thanks for the power of that love, remembering that it is the greatest gift that we give each other, and that God gives us.

29 JUNE

Weddings
Borrowed

A young couple are in a bakery, asking about cakes for special occasions. The assistant shows them a splendid iced cake for £74. The young woman mentions that it is for their wedding, whereupon the assistant, with a flourish, produces an identical cake – but this is a *'wedding* cake' because it has a pink ribbon round it and a plastic bride and groom on top. And it costs £290. The same experience is repeated in a florists, and when the couple attempt to book a band: as the husband-to-be tries to go for the much cheaper, non-wedding option, his tearful fiancée is persuaded to pay the extra money because it is her 'special day'.[24]

This series of comedy sketches neatly illustrates a real problem for couples planning a wedding: the enormous cost. 'Something borrowed' all too often means money, as couples and their families get into debt in order to pay for the perfect wedding.

In your prayers today, remember all those preparing for a wedding and struggling to afford it:

> pray for the parents who want the best for their daughter;
>
> pray for the couple who want a day to remember;
>
> pray for the bride weighed down by the expectations of others,

by the quest for her ideal weight and the
  perfect dress;
pray for the groom, whose friends expect
  a stag night they'll never forget
and pray for all those who are daunted
  by lists and plans and mounting bills.

30 JUNE

Weddings
Blue

Weddings are not always a joyful occasion for everyone. In families where there has been bereavement or divorce, a couple's happy day can re-open old wounds and cause bitter regrets. There are the practical and emotional problems of including both ex-partners and new step-families. Sometimes the sheer impossibility of keeping everybody happy can feel overwhelming.

In your prayers today, remember those who can't feel the joy of a wedding:

> Lord of love and laughter,
> while you cherish the newly-weds,
> may you also comfort the rest:
> the sad and angry ones,
> who feel let down by life and love;
> the couples in crisis,
> who are struggling to hold on to love;
> the lonely, who feel love has passed them by.
> May you be near those present who miss
>   loved ones they have lost,
> and with those ex-partners who have stayed
>   away,
> knowing that this day's happiness excludes
>   them.
> And may the light of your love shine in the
>   lives of all.
> Amen.

July

1 JULY

Waiting for the call

At this time of year, in churches and cathedrals all over the country, men and women are being ordained as deacons and priests. During their journey towards ordination, they will have been encouraged to talk about their vocation, their calling to ministry. In general use, 'vocation' is a term reserved for the pious or the artistically gifted; but every one of us has a calling. Throughout your life you are called to be the best *you* can possibly be, and as you make decisions along the way you may sometimes feel powerfully drawn towards what turns out to be the right path for you.

In a time of quiet, open your mind and heart to receive God's call to become more fully the person he made you. Simply wait and listen, perhaps with your hands open before you, ready to receive.

2 JULY

Hearing the call

> Here I am, Lord. Is it I, Lord?
> I have heard you calling in the night.
> I will go, Lord, if you lead me.
> I will hold your people in my heart.[1]

This hymn is sung regularly at ordination services because it vividly describes the experience of hearing and responding to God's call. I'm sure there are people who have felt summoned as if by a voice in the night, out of the blue. Others hear their call in the words of a close friend, or the text of a newspaper article. I have seen friends become more fully and truly themselves by falling in love, by becoming parents or by finding a fulfilling career. For many people, a call gathers more slowly, building and strengthening over the years before it is clearly recognised and answered.

Today, rest in a time of quiet and simply repeat the words, 'Here I am, Lord. Is it I, Lord?' Let them rest in your mind as a question in search of an answer. As you carry on with your day, consider whether God may be calling to you in a sudden change or unexpected encounter, or through your usual round of interations, conversations and experiences.

3 JULY

Following the call

I once heard a priest describe what it was like to answer his call to ministry, when he was tempted by other career paths. He compared it to being invited down a long corridor, like a hospital corridor, closed off at intervals by heavy fire doors. He didn't want to go down it, so tried a series of more tempting corridors. As he tried each one, some doors opened easily but others hardly moved and some were locked. Some slammed in his face. Eventually, he felt himself called back to the first corridor, and tried it in weary resignation. Suddenly, door after door flew open before him as he encountered each interview, assessment and spiritual challenge, until he found his way clear to ordination. That was how he knew he was on the right path.

Not all of us may be blessed with such a clear call to the path in life which is right for us. In a quiet time, consider the big decisions you have made in life and reflect on how you were called in the right direction. What affirmation did your choice receive? Bring before God any decisions you need to make now, and ask for his call to lead you.

4 JULY

Independence Day

> We hold these truths to be self-evident, that all men are created equal, that they are endowed by their Creator with certain unalienable Rights, that among these are Life, Liberty and the Pursuit of Happiness.[2]

Today the United States of America celebrates the day it freed itself from British rule in 1776. These words come from the Declaration of Independence and they echo down the years.

In your prayers today, remember all those who want to seize with both hands their rights to life, liberty and the pursuit of happiness:

> those who are in prison;
>
> those who are held without trial;
>
> those who are enslaved;
>
> those who are subjected to forced labour;
>
> those who are confined by ill health;
>
> those who have lost their independence in old age,
>
> and all those known to you who are denied their right to freedom.

5 JULY

Independent

Playgrounds today are not like the places I remember from childhood. They are carefully fenced off to keep out dogs and their mess; under the swings and slide there is bouncy tarmac to cushion any falls. The see-saw has a rubber stop under each seat so that children can't 'bump' each other, as I used to do to my little brother until his teeth rattled. In some playgrounds there are rules against lone adults, unattended by children. Then there are the extreme protective measures, such as one school's ban on the wearing of scarves in its playground, because of the danger of accidental strangulation. As a society we are becoming increasingly risk-averse, and as a parent I feel the tension between wanting to protect my children and wanting them to experience the world as it really is – hard tarmac and all – so that they can learn and grow into independent, responsible adults.

As a preparation for prayer today, look around you for signs of the careful, protective society we live in: are we being caring or over-protective? In prayer, bring before God your own feelings about the tension between protection and personal freedom.

6 JULY
Freedom train

> This old Freedom Train is such a
> long time in a comin',
> there ain't no one can't afford it,
> so you'd better climb on board it,
> give me that . . . freedom![3]

The spirituals sung by slaves in America expressed their longing for freedom and also, it is said, contained coded messages for other slaves about the underground railroad which helped to liberate many. Slavery today goes under the name of 'people trafficking': for many desperate people, the 'Freedom Train' is a lorry or ship's container which carries them not to the better life they had hoped for, but to sexual exploitation or hard labour. This slavery is supposed to pay off their debt to the traffickers.

In your prayers today, remember all those people who are bought and sold:

> the young children bought as cheap
>   labour to make our chocolate and clothes;
> the women and girls forced to sell their
>   bodies for sex;
> the young adults purchased as an expendable workforce;
> all those desperate to escape to the First
>   World by any means possible.

Pray for them, and pray for yourself, that your eyes might be opened to the slavery which we all support and endorse unless we oppose and condemn it.

7 JULY

Freedom bound

Tony Last is an amateur explorer who is lost in the Brazilian rainforest. Alone and feverish, he is cared for in a native village which is governed by an Englishman, Mr Todd, who asks Tony to read to him from his beloved collection of Dickens' novels. The days stretch into weeks, and every day Tony reads but becomes more impatient about finding his way home. However, he knows he will die in the jungle if he attempts to cross it alone, and none of the native Indians will assist him without their governor's permission. Mr Todd, who is himself illiterate, is in no hurry to lose such a talented reader of Dickens, so when a British search party comes looking for Tony, Mr Todd drugs him so he can be kept hidden for two days. He sends the would-be rescuers away with Tony's watch, which they take as proof of his death. No one will come looking for him again, and this is where the story leaves him.[4] It is a chilling image of a strange kind of life imprisonment: Tony's host is always courteous, his physical needs are met and he is free to leave at any time – but he is trapped as surely as if he were behind bars.

Today, bring before God those people in the 'Free World' whose liberty is an illusion:

> pray for those who are trapped by debt,
> who can see no way out of increasing
> interest and endless repayments;

for those in the 'poverty trap',
where anything more than a low-paid job
means the loss of vital benefits;
for those confined to ghettos and run-
down estates
and for all those who feel there is no
escape.

8 JULY
Escape

Three years after the Berlin Wall came down, I travelled round Eastern Europe and visited Colditz Castle. It was quite hard to find, because to the locals it was just another former Nazi prison, not a place to be advertised with great pride. Apart from a small museum in the town and a shy young woman who showed us round, there was little provision for tourists. This made it all the more exciting: the vast, crumbling castle, built on solid rock, had not been primped and reconstructed. There were rusty tins and tools from the war years lying about, as if the prisoners had just left them there. One of the tunnels they had dug was open in the middle of the floor, with no fencing or grilles. In the museum, we saw the perfect replicas of Nazi rubber stamps they had carved out of the soles of their boots. There were full German uniforms with correct insignia, made from materials which had been begged, borrowed and stolen. Best of all were the eyewitness accounts of the glider, lovingly constructed in a concealed attic from bits of wood and strips of linen. I was very moved by this evidence of the prisoners' ingenuity, audacity and sheer, bloody-minded determination to escape.

In a time of quiet, reflect on that primal urge for freedom. Give thanks for the freedom which you enjoy, and pray that you might use that great gift wisely.

9 JULY
Flower festivals

At this time of year, many churches host their annual flower festival. This involves a phenomenal amount of planning, preparation and organisation by dedicated volunteers. Whenever I go to admire the themed displays, I am reminded of how flowers can speak to us. In the past, and especially during the Victorian age, flowers were symbols which could be combined in a painting or a posy to convey a coded message. For me, flowers are mementoes of childhood: I remember the smell of sweetpeas, the soft petals of my grandmother's roses, the buttercups I held under my sister's chin to see if she liked butter and the handfuls of cherry blossom I gathered on the way home from school.

In your prayers today, perhaps as you contemplate some favourite flowers in a vase or in your garden, give thanks for the beauty and usefulness of flowers, and bring before God the ways in which flowers speak to you.

10 JULY
Red rose

However much we have forgotten the coded language of flowers today, the red rose is still a popular symbol of romantic love. The ardent boyfriend splashes out on a dozen; single blooms are hawked around pubs and clubs on Valentine's Day; poor immigrant workers sell them by the bucketful to commuters waiting at traffic lights. Unfortunately, these cut flowers can fade quickly, often without even opening all their petals. They speak more eloquently of transient passion than true love. I prefer this image of a still-growing rose:

> Friendship is the breathing rose, with
> sweets in every fold.[5]

This is the kind of love, based on real understanding and closeness, which keeps on growing and giving.

In your prayers today, give thanks for this kind of love, and for those with whom you share it.

11 JULY
White lily

If you look at paintings of angels or the Virgin Mary, particularly from the Victorian period, then you are very likely to find a spray of white lilies somewhere in the picture. The lily has long been used as a symbol of purity. It is mentioned by Jesus as an example of simple, natural beauty which is received from God, rather than achieved by human work and worry: 'Consider the lilies of the field, how they grow; they neither toil nor spin, yet I tell you, even Solomon in all his glory was not clothed like one of these.'[6]

In your prayers today, consider the lily. Bring before God all the ways in which the messy business of living takes you far away from this ideal of purity and simplicity. Name the complex demands of daily life which can leave you feeling muddled and grubby, and confess your own need for purification, perhaps repeating these words from Psalm 51:

> Create in me a clean heart, O God,
> and put a new and right spirit
>   within me.[7]

12 JULY

Rosemary

> There's rosemary; that's for remembrance
> – pray, love, remember. And there is
> pansies, that's for thoughts.[8]

These words are spoken by a grieving girl in a play written over four hundred years ago, but the sprigs of rosemary which often accompany Remembrance Day poppies show that this floral symbolism is still with us. This evergreen herb, with its lingering, bitter-sweet scent, seems an appropriate emblem of remembrance.

Today, find a sprig of rosemary and rub it in your hands to release the scent. In a time of quiet, bring before God those lost loved ones whom you remember with sadness and with joy. As the fragrance of rosemary fills the air, let your mind fill with the memories you shared and thank God for them.

13 JULY
Pansy

> Sometimes I sits and thinks, and
> sometimes I just sits.[9]

The pansy gets its name from *pensée*, the French word for 'thought', presumably because the flat petals form a kind of face which seems to bend forward attentively, giving the flower a thoughtful air.

For your prayers today, find a quiet place to sit, perhaps outside among the flowers. Sit still and let your thoughts flow out like water draining from a bath, until at last you are just sitting. Offer to God that time of quiet, unthinking stillness.

14 JULY

Dutch flower painting

When a flower festival is over, the dismantled displays are a sorry sight, with drooping heads, browning leaves and petals turning to crêpe. The blooms which are heading for the compost heap remind me of the Dutch flower paintings of the seventeenth century. These still-life arrangements were partly a celebration of the tulip, which was then an exotic novelty. A typical flower painting from this time shows an exuberant mass of flowers bursting out of a vase. There are several blowsy tulips with stripy petals and some full-blown roses dangling their heavy heads and almost tipping out of the vase. Butterflies sip nectar and there are snails and caterpillars crawling among the tousled leaves. There is a sense of heavy, over-ripe sweetness which is bordering on decay. These paintings served as a warning against worldly vanity by showing the transience of beauty and the inevitability of corruption and death.

Today, try an active form of prayer by making your own floral picture of death and – in this case – rebirth. Pick a dandelion or two and place them in an egg cup without water. They will wither and die over the next few days, but keep them and they will open up once more, this time as dandelion clocks, full of the seeds of new life. In a time of quiet, give thanks for the promise of new life which belongs to us all.

15 JULY

ACTS
Adoration

The acronym ACTS stands for the four major elements of prayer: adoration, confession, thanksgiving and supplication (humble request). I still find this helpful as one way of thinking about prayer.

> And I pray that you, being rooted and established in love, may have power, together with all the saints, to grasp how wide and long and high and deep is the love of Christ, and to know this love that surpasses knowledge – that you may be filled to the measure of all the fullness of God.[10]

We are not used to adoring. We are comfortable with liking, admiring and loving others, but adoration? That is something else. It involves being completely focused on the other, and entirely forgetful of ourselves. Paul's words here breathe such adoration. He seems wholly absorbed by his vision of Christ's love for us.

In your prayers this week, re-read this passage and take time to let it sink in. Be still, and seek to lose yourself in his loving presence.

16 JULY

ACTS
Confession

> I confess to almighty God,
> and to you, my brothers and sisters,
> that I have sinned through my own fault
> (*All strike their breast*)
> in my thoughts and in my words,
> in what I have done,
> and in what I have failed to do.[11]

This particular form of communal confession appeals to me because it is so comprehensive: it is addressed to God and our fellow human beings, and it embraces all possible kinds of wrongdoing. I also find the action helpful: as a basic, often instinctive gesture we use to emphasise *me* and *mine*, it helps make the confession personal and immediate.

In a time of quiet, try saying through these words of confession slowly and deliberately. Let nothing be left behind: name it all in God's presence and pray for his forgiveness, knowing that it is yours even before you ask for it.

17 JULY

ACTS
Thanksgiving

> Be still,
> for the glory of the Lord
> is shining all around.[12]

As very small children, we are taught to say thank you: it is one of our simplest and most important lessons. For me, coming to faith was all about wanting to say thank you to God for the many good things I had received and taken for granted.

In your prayers, look around you and reflect with thankfulness on the glory of God, which does indeed shine all around us. It shines in the great blessings of our lives, and gleams in the little things such as a friend's act of kindness, or the unexpected generosity of a stranger. It even glimmers in the dark corners where we at first find only pain and sadness. Be still, and give thanks.

18 JULY

ACTS
Supplication

It has been said that when we pray, we sometimes expect God to operate like a vending machine: we insert the appropriate prayer and wait for whatever we ordered. Our prayers can start to resemble shopping lists.

Today, simply rest in the presence of the One who knows all your needs and worries, before you name them. As a different way of making your prayer, hold a piece of clay or dough in your hands and let your fingers play with it and shape it in whichever way they choose. As and when you need to, call to mind the many things and people you wish to bring before God – and then leave them in his hands, to be held and shaped as you hold the clay in yours.

19 JULY

Day and night

It was very odd. We were sitting outside our tent, enjoying a game of cards before bedtime, but we kept playing for hours because it never got dark. Eventually I looked at my watch: it was one o'clock in the morning. It was a summer's evening, our first night beside a lake in northern Norway, and I had forgotten that this close to the Arctic Circle we would have twenty-four-hour daylight. I felt completely disoriented.

The separation of light from darkness, day from night, happens right at the start of the Creation story, before anything else comes into being. It remains a fundamental part of our lives, a basic clock which divides the rhythm of our days. Today, try to pray either at dawn or dusk, and thank God for this first gift of Creation, perhaps using these words:

> Lord of light and life,
> sun-shaper and moon-maker,
> thank you for radiant daylight
> and deep darkness
> and the familiar sweetness of twilight.
> May this heartbeat of my days
> remind me that my time is neither made
>   nor owned by me,
> but given, with love, by you.
> Amen.

20 JULY

Insomniac

> He suffers his desert pillow, sleeplessness
> stretching its fine, irritating sand in all
> directions.[13]

This painfully accurate description of insomnia reminds me of those people who dread nightfall because they once again have to face their inability to sleep. In your prayers today, bring before God all those who struggle through the night, trying and failing to sleep:

> those who are ill, whom pain keeps wakeful;
>
> those who fear death will come with sleep;
>
> those who are terrified of what the morning will bring;
>
> those who have nowhere safe to sleep;
>
> those who suffer from nightmares;
>
> those who can find no peace of mind,
>
> and all those known to you who are sleepless.

21 JULY

Sleep deprivation

The new parents have arrived for a birthday celebration, and in the car their baby has fallen fast asleep for the first time in what seems like days. The mother flinches at every sound that might wake him up, even a car door opening, so that eventually both parents stay sitting in the car and their hosts pass food and presents in to them – very quietly – through the windows.[14]

This comedy sketch illustrates beautifully the lengths to which exhausted parents will go just to get a bit of peace. It reminds me of many struggles in the small hours to get a fractious baby back to sleep. In your prayers today, remember all those who are deprived of sleep by circumstance, such as new parents, shift workers and those working very long hours. For them, and for all of us, say the words from the service of Compline, which ends the day:

> Save us, O Lord, while we wake,
> and watch over us as we sleep,
> that we may pass the night with Christ
> and rest in peace.[15]
> Amen.

22 JULY
Tired

Exhausted, worn out, spent, shattered, knackered, whacked: our words for 'tired' vividly describe a state in which we are used up, damaged, broken and useless.

In your prayers today, bring before God your own tiredness, perhaps using these words:

> Gentle Lord,
> I am so tired,
> I'm on my knees.
> You have promised
> relief from my weariness
> and rest for my soul;
> take these broken pieces,
> this worn-out shell,
> in your warm hands
> and make me whole.
> Amen.

23 JULY

Dreams

> I closed my eyes,
> drew back the curtain,
> to see for certain
> what I thought I knew.[16]

These words are sung by the dreamer in *Joseph and the Amazing Technicolor Dreamcoat*. They emphasise that for Joseph, dreams spoke plainly in pictures to show him the truth. His teenage dreams of stars and sheaves of corn which bowed down to him came true when his brothers prostrated themselves before him in Egypt. His interpretations of his fellow prisoners' dreams accurately foretold their fate; his reading of Pharaoh's dreams of cows and corn saved Egypt from the effects of famine.

There have been many attempts to decode the language of dreams but, for most of us, they remain a familiar enigma. In your prayers today, bring before God the dreams you can recall, whether they are strange, explicable, recurrent or frightening. Put aside your desire to know what they are about, and simply let them rest in God's presence, as they are part of you.

24 JULY
Nightmares

My children worry about having bad dreams, and often ask for prayers at bedtime to ease these fears. Sometimes gentle blessings help; at other times, it seems as if a more forceful kind of prayer is needed.

In a time of quiet, bring before God your own bad dreams, or those of someone close to you. Use these curses, and the prayer which follows them, to push these burdens away from you and into God's hands.

> Cursed be the terrors which come at night:
> cursed be the monsters and the monstrous,
> cursed be the twisted imaginings,
> cursed be the fears with no face or name.
> Lord of light,
> may you cast out the nightmares –
> the mad, the bad,
> the dangerous and the distorted –
> and let your servant depart in peace.
> Amen.

25 JULY

Deep and dreamless sleep[17]

> . . . the innocent Sleep;
> Sleep, that knits up the ravell'd sleave
>   of care,
> the death of each day's life, sore
>   labour's bath,
> balm of hurt minds, great Nature's
>   second course,
> chief nourisher in life's feast.[18]

These rapturous words are spoken by a man who cannot sleep and is clearly longing for the comfort, refreshment and renewed strength which a good night's sleep can give. Tonight, hold in your prayers a loved one who needs such sleep, and say these words of blessing:

> As the warmth of your bed enfolds you,
> may the light of Christ encircle you,
> may the love of Christ embrace you,
> may the peace of Christ encompass you
> tonight and every night.
> Amen.

26 JULY

Pilgrims and settlers

When I was twenty-two, I took part in a month-long trip, driving and camping across Scandinavia and Eastern Europe. I had never camped before, but I became very attached to the simplicity of it: all I needed for daily life was packed into one small tent and one large hold-all; as we moved on, I left nothing behind me but a square of flattened grass where my tent had been. I remember this experience when spiritual writers talk about the difference between being a pilgrim and a settler.

On the move

In a time of quiet, look around your home and reflect on the material possessions with which we are all so richly blessed. Are retailers telling us the truth when they advertise all these things as 'home *essentials*'?

> Lord, thank you for all the comforts
> and good things I possess.
> Stir a pilgrim spirit within me
> and show me what is essential
>   for my journey with you –
> and what encumbers me
> and hinders my progress.
> Give me the strength to reject those
>   things which I want but do not need.
> In Jesus' name.
> Amen.

27 JULY

Nimbys

Whenever a new development is proposed and objections are raised, someone will accuse the opposition of being Nimbys, which stands for 'not in my back yard'. I was amused recently to find extreme Nimbys described as Notes and Bananas: 'not over there either' and 'build absolutely nothing anywhere near anything'.

As a preparation for prayer, reflect on a local issue which is bringing out the Nimbys, Notes and Bananas. In North Cornwall it is wind farms; whatever it is in your community, try to suspend your own judgement and bring the matter to God in prayer. Open your mind, and listen . . .

28 JULY

In the comfort zone

When all our material needs are satisfied, we can feel cosy and cocooned – and nicely separated from the rest of the world. We don't need to depend on others for our daily bread or for a roof over our heads. At worst, this can lead to an 'I'm all right, Jack' attitude, because we are disinclined to have others depend on us for whatever it is they need: our money, our help, our time and energy.

In a time of quiet, consider your own 'comfort zone'. Pray for an understanding of those things that give you a sense of safety and comfort.

Pray for an awareness of those people or situations you have turned away from because they have called you out of your own comfortable cocoon.

29 JULY

Out of the comfort zone

Christ's ministry led him away from the centre of power towards the fringes of his society where he encountered the poor, the marginalised, the dispossessed and the outcasts.

In a time of quiet, reflect on his example and ask for forgiveness:

> Lord of the borderland,
> the wilderness and no-man's-land,
> I do not want to leave my comfort zone.
> Things which are strange and difficult
>   unnerve me:
> people who are hard to understand and love,
> fraught relationships,
> the raw neediness of others.
> I would rather not get involved,
> but I know I must – just as you did.
> Give me strength to follow your call
>   when I hear it,
> even if it makes me walk far beyond my
>   comfort zone.
> In your mercy, hear my prayer.
> Amen.

30 JULY
End of term

> We break up, we break up,
> we don't care if the school blows up,
> no more English, no more French,
> no more sitting on the old school bench!

I remember skipping out of school with my friends on the last day of term, chanting this loudly as we walked home. Now I hear my own children sing it, and I recall those feelings of pure joy and delighted anticipation of a whole six weeks' holiday ahead.

As a preparation for prayer, consider the blessing of a holiday. Perhaps you might look back at photographs of a favourite holiday, or use the time to pack for a well-earned break. In a time of quiet, thank God for the blessing of a good holiday, which was originally a 'holy day'. Give thanks for the power it has to refresh, renew and reinvigorate us.

31 JULY

Holiday

Shirley Valentine is an ordinary housewife who is stuck in a rut. She feels as if life is passing her by, and often confides in her kitchen wall as she does the washing-up. Her story, told on stage and film, is one of joyous transformation: she accepts the surprise offer of a two-week holiday in Greece, and there she rediscovers her zest for life.

In the beginning, God rested on the seventh day, and the day of rest, or Sabbath, has been part of religious observance ever since, reminding us that rest is a basic need. In your prayers today, bring before God all those who need a holiday:

> those who work long hours,
> who feel they haven't time;
>
> those who work for low wages,
> who know they can't afford it;
>
> the unemployed and self-employed,
> who feel they can't take time off;
>
> the carers in need of respite;
>
> and all those known to you
> who are worn down and worn out.

August

1 AUGUST

'Tidal'

In this poem, the priest and poet, R. S. Thomas, considers his experience of prayer as he watches waves breaking on the beach.

> The waves run up the shore
> and fall back. I run
> up the approaches of God
> and fall back.[1]

Like the running waves, a prayer habit can be changeable and inconsistent. Sometimes we pray a great deal: during a personal crisis, or when the arrival of Lent or Advent prompts us to renew our efforts. Sometimes we hardly pray at all because we are too busy, or too distracted, or life has dealt us such a painful blow that we feel too far from God to pray.

In a time of quiet, talk to God about times when it has been easy or hard to pray. Confess the obstacles – both internal and external – that hinder your open communication with God.

Consider what helps you to pray, and as the disciples asked Jesus, ask the Lord to teach you how to pray.

2 AUGUST

Breaking waves

> Rejoice always, pray without ceasing, give thanks in all circumstances: for this is the will of God in Christ Jesus for you.[2]

Thinking of prayer as waves brings to mind Paul's challenging instruction to pray constantly. Like the waves that ceaselessly wash the beach, we must come back and back again to God in prayer, however often we fall back in despair, disappointment or simple forgetfulness.

In a time of quiet, contemplate waves on a beach, in a picture or in your memory; recall the constant rhythm and the experience of different tides. Sit quietly in God's presence and let the images of waves speak to you.

3 AUGUST
Springs and neaps

I didn't understand the difference between a spring tide and a neap tide until we moved near to a beach which simply isn't there under certain tidal conditions. Spring tides make high water very high, and low water very low; neaps still have high and low water, but the difference is much less marked. When we first visited our local beach, it was a high spring tide and there was nothing between the car park and the waves but a short stretch of slippery rock. The next day, I went at low water and found a huge expanse of sand spreading from cliff to cliff. Neap tides are not so dramatic: at low tide there is a bit of beach, then the tide comes in and there is a bit less.

The R. S. Thomas poem sees prayer, like the sea, as tidal, and this image is a comforting one. It understands our despair not as the absence of prayer, but its low tide, part of the endless, inevitable ebb and flow of prayer throughout our lives, with the promise of a high spring tide to come.

In a time of quiet, bring before God those known to you who feel that their faith has died and that God has deserted them. Pray for those who feel their prayers have run dry.

May they trust that the tide will rise once more and that God's grace will inundate their lives.

4 AUGUST

Undertow

> But some twenty yards out the smooth surge gathered into enormous waves which with sudden violent acceleration came tearing in to destroy themselves upon the shingle, which they then sucked sharply downwards and backwards with a grinding roar . . . It looked as if the beach shelved very steeply, creating an undertow, each retreating wave being sucked with positive vicious violence back beneath the tall uncurling crest of its closely following successor.[3]

There is no swimming in a sea like this. It sucks you out of your depth and pulls you back again every time you try to scramble out. You could swim until you were exhausted, and still not move any closer, then drown within sight of the shore.

In your prayers today, bring before God all those who feel their lives are out of control, as if they have been sucked out to sea by the undertow:

> those struggling with mounting debts;
>
> those whose marriage and family are breaking apart;
>
> those in the grip of an addiction;
>
> those overcome by illness;
>
> those whose work seems impossibly hard,
>
> and all those known to you who are overwhelmed.

5 AUGUST
Storm

Five thousand hungry people have just been miraculously fed, and Jesus has sent the disciples off in a boat while he has some time alone to pray.

> When evening came, the boat was out on the lake, and he was alone on the land. When he saw that they were straining at the oars against an adverse wind, he came towards them early in the morning, walking on the lake. He intended to pass them by. But when they saw him walking on the lake, they thought it was a ghost and cried out; for they all saw him and were terrified. But immediately he spoke to them and said, 'Take heart, it is I; do not be afraid.' Then he got into the boat with them and the wind ceased. And they were utterly astounded.[4]

We can sympathise with these exhausted, frightened men, in an open boat all night with a stiff wind blowing against them. The scene is also a powerful image of the kind of struggles we may all have to face – those times when we feel we are fighting a losing battle and failing to control our own panic. In a time of quiet, hold in prayer all those known to you who are facing this kind of struggle, and contemplate these encouraging words from a modern priest and preacher:

But the good news that I announce to you in the name of the storm-stilling father and the storm-stilling son and the storm-stilling spirit is this. Jesus and his 'do not fear' continue to be uttered and will finally utter us beyond our fear. Quit watching the storm and listen![5]

6 AUGUST
Surfing

In almost any weather, there are surfers on our local beaches. They swim doggedly out through the churning surf, each one a bobbing black head with a bit of board in tow. Then suddenly they are standing on top of the waves, riding them, skimming along their crests and inside their long tubes with sheer confidence and exhilaration. They return to the beach flushed and eager to catch the next wave.

In your prayers today, call to mind an occasion which created in you such feelings of excitement and delight. Dwell on that moment and the emotions it stirred in you, then bring the recollection before God, sharing with him your pleasure as you do your pains. Give thanks for pure joy.

7 AUGUST

Rocks

> The stable earth, the deep salt sea
> around the old eternal rocks.[6]

For the woman in labour, there is the inescapable certainty of having to continue labouring until her baby is born; for the patient with a life-limiting disease, there is the inescapable reality of their diagnosis. This is when we come up against those immovable things in life that someone once called the eternal severities: life and death. In our circles of family and friends, many of us have experienced our lives being put on hold by the expectation of an imminent birth or death. In the face of this rock-like certainty, everything else in our lives has to move to accommodate it.

Today, offer to God in prayer all those immovable things in your life, and the lives of those close to you, about which you feel you can do nothing – except pray.

8 AUGUST
Taking root

Rocks and cliffs may look bare from a distance, but close up you can see that every crack and cranny which can serve as a foothold has become a home for something: barnacles, limpets, mussels and tenacious seaweeds, then higher up the shore there are grasses, lichens and flowers which have taken root in the cliff. In the poem, 'Tidal', R. S. Thomas sees these as symbols of faith which can take root in the most unlikely and unpromising of circumstances.

Today, reflect in thankfulness on all those occasions, great and small, which have increased your trust in God, perhaps using this prayer:

> Thanks be to God,
> miraculous Healer
> and Provider of daily bread.
> Thanks be to God,
> Creator of this fertile planet
> and Maker of the wild flower.
> Thanks be to God,
> Inspirer of world-changing charity
> and Prompter of kind words.
> Thanks be to God,
> Knitter of peace treaties
> and Mender of broken friendships.
> Thanks be to God,
> Lord of all and Lover of the least –
> even me.
> Thanks be to God, in whom I trust.
> Amen.

9 AUGUST

Bodies

At the first sign of sunshine, we go mad and start baring some flesh in shorts, sandals and swimwear. Bodies which have remained under wraps all winter are boldly displayed on beaches, and they remind me of the famous words of St Teresa:

> Christ has no body now on earth but yours,
> no hands but yours,
> no feet but yours.
>
> Yours are the eyes through which
> Christ's compassion is to look out on the world.
>
> Yours are the feet by which he is to go about doing good,
>
> and yours are the hands with which he is to bless us now.[7]

In a time of quiet, reflect on these words and let them speak to you. Open your heart and listen ...

10 AUGUST
Hands

With these hands
... I soothe the fever, cool the heat,
I lift verrucas out of feet.[8]

These lines are taken from Pam Ayres' poem, 'With These Hands', which describes the comically contrasting tasks we require our hands to perform. I often think of them and smile as I use my hands to cook the tea, wash children's hair, feed the dog and then write these prayers.

In a time of prayer, consider your hands. Bring before God all the things they have done for you and for others today, and all the things they have yet to do. Offer them to God for his blessing, using this short prayer:

Take these hands to do your work
and let your will be done.
Amen.

11 AUGUST

Feet

In the rough backstreets of Italy in the early seventeenth century, a young troublemaker called Caravaggio produced sacred paintings for some of the great churches of his time. His models were the beggars, prostitutes and malingerers among whom he lived, and his work was revolutionary because of its realism: his subjects are depicted in vivid colours, sharp light and unflinching physical detail. A recent survey of his paintings makes a fascinating observation:

> You will see grotty feet everywhere in Caravaggio's paintings, the shoddy soles of people who spend their days and nights barefoot, running or limping through dusty city streets, selling fruit or their bodies, begging alms. You see them in his Madonna of the Rosary in Vienna, in which the filthy, battered feet of the poor face us as their humble possessors kneel and raise their hands beseechingly towards black rosary beads offered by the church.[9]

However high and holy the theme, it is the grotty feet which reveal the underlying humanity of Caravaggio's art. In a time of quiet, consider your own feet. Uncover that part of yourself which, most of the time, you keep hidden from general view, and look at them with a painter's eye. Notice the uneven nails, the

continued overleaf

cracked skin, the corns, the hairy toes, the blue veins and the red heels. In your prayers, bring your feet before God as a symbol of your own humanity, the real you. Confess what you are and what you have been, trusting that God loves you and wants to make you whole and holy.

12 AUGUST

Skin

Être mal dans sa peau: to feel ill at ease, unhappy, at odds with oneself; literally, to feel 'wrong in one's skin'.

This French phrase gives unhappiness a physical reality: your skin is intimately part of you, and yet it can feel uncomfortable and wrong, like someone else's shoes.

In your prayers today, bring before God everyone who feels *mal dans sa peau*:

> those who are depressed;
>
> those who despise themselves;
>
> those who are suicidal;
>
> those who are driven by mental anguish to cut their own skin;
>
> those who feel they are ugly or fat or old and cannot love the skin they are in,
>
> and all those known to you who simply wish they were someone else.

13 AUGUST

Eyes

I remember an Army recruitment advert which gave a soldier's-eye view of a crisis. During a peace-keeping mission somewhere in Africa, an argument between armed guerrillas was spiralling towards violent chaos. The soldier through whom we viewed the scene was face to face with a very angry man who was ignoring any attempts to calm him down. Suddenly, the soldier's hand reached up to remove his own sunglasses. Our view brightened, and we saw the man taken aback by the change. He paused, then spoke altogether more calmly and reasonably. Once he could look into the soldier's eyes, he began talking to a human being, not an anonymous figure of authority.

In a time of quiet, give thanks for the gift of our eyes:

> Creator God,
> thank you for these windows of our soul,
> through which we can read the changing
>   weather of the heart.
> In another's eyes we see the sunshine
>   and the passing clouds.
> When words fail us,
> our eyes reveal the breaking storms,
> the deluge of tears and the fire of love.
> Word of God, who uttered us into being,
> though vision may be weak or sight
>   failing,
> thank you for the lasting eloquence of
>   our eyes.
> Amen.

14 AUGUST

Foetal

There is a painting which features a naked young man sitting on a flat rock by the sea. He is curled in on himself, head down and knees drawn tightly against his body. The painting is called 'Misery', and the man is showing his desperate need for comfort and self-protection by reverting to the position of a foetus in the womb. It is a position we naturally adopt when we are at our most child-like and vulnerable, often when we are asleep and sometimes if we are extremely frightened or in distress.

In your prayers today, curl yourself into a foetal position and bring to mind all those known to you who are suffering in body, mind or spirit. As you sit in that defensive, self-hugging posture, name before God all those who are in desperate need of comfort and healing. Pray that they might feel his loving arms around them and know his restoring power.

15 AUGUST

Open hands

Opening the hands, palm upwards, is a part of the body's language we all instinctively use and understand. It expresses openness and honesty: it says, 'Look – no weapon. I come in peace,' or, 'Nothing up my sleeve – what you see is what you get.' It says, 'I'm telling you the truth,' and, 'Trust me.' The open palm is also a gesture of offering and receiving: for two people to shake hands, one must make the invitation with an open palm and the other must accept it in the same way. In some forms of meditation, the palms are kept open and upwards in a receptive position; in some churches, hands are raised in worship and thanksgiving.

In a time of quiet, try using the language of your hands in prayer. Kneel or sit cross-legged and open your hands in front of you. Rest in God's presence and let your hands stay open, revealing all, trusting all and ready to receive.

16 AUGUST

Prostrate

Lying face down on the floor in front of someone is a gesture of utter self-abasement. It belongs mostly in the courts of kings and potentates, although I am reminded of it every time I have to speak sternly to my dog and she prostrates herself at my feet, acknowledging my status as her 'pack leader'. In the language of the body, whether human or animal, the action says, 'I am entirely inferior to you, and I acknowledge your power over me.'

In a time of quiet, call to mind the stern words from Psalm 46:

> Be still, and know that I am God![10]

When you feel settled in the stillness, lie down on the floor with your arms stretched out. Feel the strangeness of the position; acknowledge how vulnerable and, perhaps, humbled it makes you feel, and let your body say your prayer for you.

17 AUGUST

Open arms

Tucked between London's Hatton Garden and the Gray's Inn Road is the church of St Alban's, Holborn. It was built in the middle of a Victorian slum – said to be the inspiration for Fagin's world in *Oliver Twist* – and partly rebuilt after the Blitz. Whatever I expected to find the first time I walked through its small red-brick courtyard and low arched door, it was not the radiantly beautiful mural which covers the length and breadth of the wall behind the altar.[11] In vivid rainbow colours it depicts scores of figures, from imprisoned sinners to angels and saints. God the Father sits above them all; God the Holy Spirit hovers as a golden youth and a dove with spreading wings. In the very centre is God the Son. His arms are outstretched and at first it seems as if he is still on the Cross: yet this is the Risen Christ, bearing the wounds but no longer the nails, and his arms reach out to all of us in welcome and love.

Today, find a representation of Christ on the Cross which you can use as a focus for your prayers. Whether it is a painting, crucifix, icon or statue, hold it before you as you sit in God's presence. Look at the open arms, nailed into a gesture of welcome and compassionate embrace. Let that sign of Christ's all-embracing love speak to you in prayer.

18 AUGUST

Laughter

- Knock, knock!
- *Who's there?*
- The Interrupting Cow.
- *The Interrupting Cow wh –*
- MOO!

My children made each other laugh and laugh with this joke, and no amount of repetition seemed to diminish their delight in the perfectly timed punchline.

In your prayers today, call to mind the things and people that really make you laugh, and give thanks for the joy of laughter:

> for the witty friends who always cheer you up;
>
> for the shared laughter that binds friends together;
>
> for the remembered jokes and funny stories that families tell each other;
>
> for the satisfaction of a belly laugh,
>
> the delight of a giggle
>
> and the wonderful liberation of out-of-control, tear-wiping, breath-snatching hilarity.

19 AUGUST
Satire

> A young healthy child, well nursed, is, at a year old, a most delicious, nourishing, and wholesome food, whether stewed, roasted, baked, or boiled; and I make no doubt that it will equally serve in a fricassee or a ragout.[12]

In this essay in 1729, Jonathan Swift satirised the brutal attitude of the English towards the Irish poor. Its full title is: 'A Modest Proposal for Preventing the Children of Poor People in Ireland from Being a Burden to Their Parents or Country, and for Making Them Beneficial to the Public'. After expressing great concern for starving Irish families, he proposes that the best solution would be cannibalism. If the poor sold their children to the rich as food, the problems of poverty, starvation and overpopulation would be solved. He describes his plan in calm and reasonable detail, shocking the reader into an understanding of the real hardships of the Irish and the callousness of the English ruling class.

This is true satire, employing ironic wit to form a moral judgement in the audience. Since the politically active 1960s, modern satire has enjoyed a boom period on television, from *That Was The Week That Was* to *Spitting Image*, *Brass Eye* and *Have I Got News For You*. It may be silly or challenging, occasionally brutal and shocking. In a time of quiet today, reflect on the ability of comedy to make you think. Call to mind the things that make you laugh, and ask God to speak to you through them.

20 AUGUST
Controversial comedy

It is AD 33. Brian has attracted a huge crowd outside his mother's house in a back street of Jerusalem. The crowd mistakenly believes Brian is the messiah, and he is trying in vain to persuade them otherwise. He urges them not to follow the herd, but to behave like individuals who can make up their own minds:

> Brian: You're all different!
> Crowd: Yes, we ARE all different!
> Man in crowd: I'm not . . .[13]

This delightfully silly exchange from *The Life of Brian* pokes fun at mindless following, and is typical of this film's comedy. It was famously condemned as blasphemous when it was released in 1979, and was banned by several councils. However, I think the butt of the jokes is not Christ or Christians, but witless credulity and flawed humanity. The Monty Python team laugh at all those who are so keen to believe in something that they will believe in anything.

In a time of quiet, call to mind a joke, comedy sketch or film which has shocked or offended you, or which made you laugh while it offended others. Share your reaction with God in prayer and, through your feelings, open your heart to listen to him.

21 AUGUST

Laughing at God

Abraham was ninety-nine years old, and his wife, Sarah, was ninety and childless. When God told Abraham that Sarah would bear him a son, 'Abraham fell on his face and laughed'.[14] When Sarah heard the news, she laughed even more:

> Sarah laughed to herself, saying, 'After I have grown old, and my husband is old, shall I have pleasure?' The Lord said to Abraham, 'Why did Sarah laugh, and say, "Shall I indeed bear a child, now that I am old?" Is anything too wonderful for the Lord? At the set time I will return to you, in due season, and Sarah shall have a son.' But Sarah denied, saying, 'I did not laugh'; for she was afraid. He said, 'Oh yes, you did laugh.'[15]

This is the laughter of disbelief and denial: neither Abraham nor Sarah can comprehend that God could accomplish anything so miraculous. In your prayers today, name before God those people and situations known to you that seem to need a miracle. Remember that laughter and God's reply: *Is anything too wonderful for the Lord?*

22 AUGUST
Laughing at yourself

When I have to explain to my children the difference between laughing *with* someone and laughing *at* them, I recall a famously cringe-worthy moment of television history. This was the appearance of David Icke, as self-proclaimed son of God, on the *Wogan* show. Earnest and serene, he explained his messianic vision to an astonished audience. The laughter bubbled up, and David Icke smiled as Terry Wogan pointed out that the audience was not laughing with him, but at him.

We will always get ourselves into trouble if we take ourselves too seriously. One of the most sane and balanced things we can do is learn to laugh at ourselves, with all our flaws and failings. In a time of quiet, bring before God those aspects of yourself which, if you take a step back and look at them, make you smile or even snort with laughter at your own ridiculousness. Look at yourself as if to say, 'What am I *like*?!' Let the laughter be a release as you hand these things over to God, for his healing power to transform.

23 AUGUST
Between the lines

'George – don't do that.'[16]

I love the comedy of Joyce Grenfell, and especially her Nursery School monologues, in which a resolutely cheerful teacher has her patience tested by her class of little darlings, none of whom we ever see or hear. We only hear the increasing strain in her voice as she tries to remain jolly despite the rebellious Sidney and the undoubtedly revolting George, who will keep doing something he shouldn't. The power of her comedy lies in what is left unsaid, and in what our imaginations fill in between the lines.

In a time of quiet, pray for your ears to be opened to what is left unsaid in the conversations you have today. In between the lines of the cheery anecdote or the brisk chat, is there another story being told? Pray for ears to hear what people perhaps mean to say, but don't, and pray for the sensitivity to respond appropriately.

24 AUGUST

Fear
Jaws

The following prayers have been inspired by the 'blockbuster', a summer tradition in cinemas which has established itself over the last thirty years. The ingredients are simple: big budget, big stars, huge special effects and mass appeal. These examples of popular storytelling tend to play on our primal instincts, and none more so than the original blockbuster, *Jaws*. Everything about this film is direct and designed to terrify. Its tag line was simply, 'Don't go in the water.' The famous music was based on a bare two-note sequence which still sends shivers down the spine. Remember the poster: at the top there is a lone swimmer, splashing happily on the surface, while through the cross-section of the deep sea beneath her a truly enormous shark is surging upwards, its mouth bristling with teeth and open in readiness . . .

The basic story-line, in which a monster is hunted down and killed, is as old as stories themselves. It is *Beowulf*, it is Theseus and the Minotaur, it is our old fireside tales of giants and dragons. In such stories, through fantasy and imagery, we explore some of our deepest fears and most basic instincts. In your prayers today, bring before God the things which frighten you, perhaps by recalling a film or story which particularly

continued overleaf

touched you. Name those fears, and try saying this old prayer for the evening:

> Lighten our darkness,
> we beseech thee, O Lord,
> and by thy great mercy defend us
> from all perils and dangers of this night;
> for the love of thy only Son,
> our Saviour Jesus Christ.
> Amen.[17]

25 AUGUST

Freedom
Pirates of the Caribbean

> Jack: That's what a ship is, you know. Not just a keel and a hull and a deck and sails. That's what a ship needs...but what a ship is – what the *Black Pearl* really is...is freedom.[18]

For Captain Jack Sparrow, freedom has a shape and a name: it is his precious ship, the *Black Pearl*. His attempts to reclaim it drive the film forward, and the ending is deeply satisfying because, at last, we see him take the helm of the *Pearl* and head for the horizon.

This longing for freedom can overtake us all, but few of us, perhaps, can so clearly identify what it is that will make us free. In your prayers today, bring before God those who long to escape but don't know how:

> those who feel driven to suicide;
>
> those who try to escape through drink and drugs;
>
> those who find freedom in cyberspace;
>
> those whose longing to escape their daily lives is tritely described as 'a mid-life crisis',
>
> and all those known to you who feel trapped.

26 AUGUST

Home
Gladiator

This muscular film, which single-handedly revived the 'swords and sandals' epic, is shot through with the hero's longing for home. A repeated dream-sequence shows Maximus returning to his farm, embracing his wife and son and running his hands through the ripe corn growing on his own land. The dream turns to nightmare when we see the scene replayed in reality and it is not Maximus riding through the cornfields but soldiers bent on rape and murder. He finds fame as a gladiator in Rome, but he does not get his heart's desire until he is killed in the ring; in death we see him finding his wife and son among the corn once more.

In your prayers today, remember all those who long for home:

> the refugee who saw his house destroyed by a natural disaster, longing for something which doesn't exist;
>
> the asylum-seeker driven from her home by war, surviving in a camp and worrying about who may be living in her home now;
>
> those who, through choice or circumstance, are a long way from home:
>
> the soldiers and the aid-workers,
>
> the travellers and the missing,
>
> the homesick and the homeless.

27 AUGUST

Change
Back to the Future

Marty is part of a dysfunctional family. His father is a weak loser who is bullied at work and his mother is overweight and depressed, old before her time. When he takes part in a time travel experiment, he finds himself back in the 1950s when his parents were about to meet at High School. He inadvertently changes the course of history and has to struggle to get his parents together for their first kiss before he writes himself out of existence. Of course, he succeeds, but when he returns to the present day he finds there has been a transformation: his father is now a successful author and his parents are a glamorous, happy pair.

As a piece of wish-fulfilment fantasy, this film cannot be bettered. How wonderful to be able to return to a critical point in the past and change our own history for the better! In a time of quiet, bring before God those turning points in your own life which you wish now had turned out differently. Hold the past in prayer and offer up the future, with its crossroads yet to come, entrusting all to the God who encompasses time and space.

28 AUGUST
Sandcastles

I watched my daughter making her sandcastle on the beach, labouring over it all day high up on the sand. She carefully dug and maintained the moat, shoring it up with pebbles; finally, she dug a channel which stretched out hopefully in the direction of the distant surf. At long last, as the beach emptied around us at the end of the day, the sea flooded into the moat and completed her handiwork, and she danced with delight.

Today, hold this image in prayer:

> Thank you, Lord,
> for such faithful labour, such perfect trust.
> Inspire us to stretch out to you in our prayers
> and to trust that,
> however humbly made they may be,
> our prayers are a channel
> through which your grace may flood
>   our lives.
> Amen.

29 AUGUST
Windbreaks

Last summer, it seemed that the beaches were dominated by windbreaks. They had become windbreak estates, with many people cordoning off their 'own' bit of beach with an unbroken circular fence of at least six of the things. These folk could not have been able to see the sea, the cliffs or anybody else on the beach – just their own small, sandy territory with their own people on it.

In your prayers, reflect on the ways in which we all fence ourselves in: the personal comfort zones we carefully preserve; the mental barriers we erect between ourselves and others, especially those who make us feel awkward, resentful or afraid. Confess your need for the sense of security these fences give – and pray for the strength to reach out to others who are left outside.

30 AUGUST
Beachcombing

The late Cornish playwright, Nick Darke, was a serious beachcomber. A recent documentary about his life explored his living catalogue of finds – everything from exotic seeds and tropical hard woods to tiny numbered pieces of plastic which he traced to individual fishermen in Newfoundland.

In a time of quiet, recollect your own experience of beachcombing, and remember the *attentiveness* this activity requires: patience, a sharp eye and a minute consideration of the different patterns on this pebble, or that piece of driftwood. In your prayers today, try to turn such attentiveness to the needs of those around you. Remember before God the pressing, urgent needs which are impossible to ignore, and the small, often unconsidered ways in which people you know need your prayers.

31 AUGUST

'Not Waving But Drowning'

This is the title of a devastating little poem by Stevie Smith, which voices the thoughts of a drowned man. He was thought of as a bit of a joker; when he swam out of his depth, his frantic signals for help had been misinterpreted as high-spirited clowning. His last thought is:

> 'I was much too far out all my life
> and not waving but drowning.'[19]

In a time of quiet, consider the display of cheerfulness which all of us can use to hide our real needs. Pray for the discernment to see when others are not waving but drowning, and ask for the strength to offer a helping hand.

September

1 SEPTEMBER

Roots

'Tree of Life' was the theme of the first Greenbelt Festival I visited, and it has inspired the following prayer suggestions.

We all have roots. They are our origins: the people who nurtured us and the places and cultural influences which formed us. Some of us honour our roots; some of us spend our lives trying to deny or escape them, but whatever our feelings towards them, our roots are part of us.

In your prayers, reflect on your roots and what they mean to you. If you can, visit a place you knew well as a child and spend some quiet time there. Alternatively, find those photographs that have been tucked away for years: your childhood home, your first day at school, your parents with you as a baby. Let the memories well up, perhaps with some tears, and hold those feelings in prayer, knowing that God is with you, and that he hears your prayer.

2 SEPTEMBER

Shoots

Last autumn's pruning left our apple tree looking bare and dead – nothing but dry sticks all winter. But in the spring, strong green shoots came, forcing themselves out of every cranny and straining towards the sun.

In your prayers, ask for God's blessing on new growth: offer up the new directions which your own life may be taking, and pray for their flourishing in a godward direction.

Pray for the new directions which are being explored by people close to you:

> the child finding new talents through school;
>
> the teenager off to university;
>
> the parents whose children have recently left home;
>
> the newly retired
>
> and the widowed.

Pray for those who feel like dead wood in body, mind or spirit, that they might be filled with new life and hope.

3 SEPTEMBER

Fruits

The flowers and fruits of our world are a powerful reminder of God's grace. Nature gives them to us in rich abundance, for our pleasure and our use, not just once but year after year. They also remind me of some advice given to me as a young Christian, which has stayed with me through our many house-moves: 'Blossom where you're planted.'

In a time of quiet, consider where you are planted: which relationships are you part of, and which communities? We are all planted in a family and in our immediate neighbourhood; many of us are also planted in a church, school or workplace. Reflect on the part you play in these different settings, and open your heart and mind to God's will for you. In your prayers, ask: how can I blossom here? How can I express something of the generosity of God's creation through my own life? Ask and listen...

4 SEPTEMBER

Tree of Life

A mature oak tree sustains something like a thousand different species, ranging from fungi and insects to squirrels and owls. A thousand lives, dependent on each other and the great old tree which connects them all. It is all too easy to forget, as we sit within our own four walls and travel about in our own private cars, that our own lives are connected with each other and with the world we inhabit. Today, pray for your eyes to be opened with a new awareness of these connections:

> Nurturing God, thank you
> for the rich interrelation of our lives,
> for the ever-increasing connections
> that bind us to each other
> and to our living world.
> Show me what I can do to honour these relationships;
> help me to love other people in their vulnerability,
> and guide me in caring for our fragile earth.
> Amen.

5 SEPTEMBER

<u>Harvest Festival</u>
Cornucopia

Harvest Festival is celebrated this month, and churches and school halls are being decorated in traditional fashion: arrangements of flowers, fruit and vegetables; a loaf in the shape of a sheaf of corn; piles of edible offerings at the front, ranging from home-grown marrows to out-of-date tinned peaches. As the pile of food grows, it resembles a cornucopia, the mythical 'horn of plenty' which gave whatever was desired. In classical paintings, it often appears as a goat's horn brimming with harvest produce.

As a preparation for prayer today, look around your home, and especially in your kitchen cupboards. Appreciate how much you have, reflecting that if you are not starving, you are richer than many in this world. In a time of quiet, give thanks for having plenty, or more than enough, or simply enough.

6 SEPTEMBER

Hoard

All be safely gathered in,
ere the winter storms begin.[1]

Whenever there is news of a looming fuel shortage, our natural hoarding instinct kicks in. Intellectually, we know that the sensible thing is for us all to ration our fuel intake so that there will be enough to go around, but faced with the prospect of doing without, we feel compelled to stockpile our own supplies, like squirrels hoarding nuts for winter.

In your prayers today, confess your own tendency to hoard. Perhaps you appreciate the comfort of having your family's history around you, in overflowing boxes in the attic. Maybe you care for your family by being practically equipped for any eventuality. Perhaps you simply want the basic reassurance of having plenty. Whatever form it takes, share your hoarding instinct with God and let him speak to you through it.

7 SEPTEMBER

Farming

I had never really thought much about farming. I enjoyed the fields and the hedgerows that farmers maintained, although I was less keen on cows. All that changed in 2001 when we were living in rural Devon and the foot and mouth crisis struck. All the country walks we knew were blocked by big 'Infection Control' signs. Any journey to town, or the coast, took us past fields where the bloated, stinking corpses of cows were piled high, their legs sticking straight up in the air. When they began to burn them, the sea winds carried the smoke across the countryside, and what should have been a fresh breeze was filled with the stench of a rancid barbecue. The sights and smells of that summer were a physical reminder of how many farmers' lives had been blighted.

In your prayers today, remember all those who farm for a living:

> those who want to hand on their farm to their children;
>
> those who are trying to diversify in order to make ends meet;
>
> those who are struggling against high costs and low prices;
>
> those whose livelihood is threatened by disease;
>
> those who are working to satisfy the supermarkets

and those who are trying to compete
  against them;
those who spend their lives balancing the
care of their farm with care for the
  environment,
and all those on whom we depend for
  our daily bread.

8 SEPTEMBER

Seasonal produce

The supermarkets have always offered us whatever we wanted, whenever we wanted it – even strawberries in December; however, we are beginning to rediscover the seasonal nature of our food. Farmers' markets and organic vegetable boxes encourage us to eat what is good, local and in season. TV chefs celebrate the delights of seasonal dining, from the first new potatoes of spring to the sweet berries of summer and the freshly caught game of autumn.

In a time of quiet, consider the treats which are ours with the turning of the seasons:

> Loving and giving Father,
> thank you for this good earth
> which nurtures and nourishes us,
> and for the good things
> that come to us in their season.
> Give me the grace to enjoy the fruits
>   of today
> and the faith to trust in your provision
>   for tomorrow.
> Amen.

9 SEPTEMBER

Back to school
Uniform

In the film *The Rebel*, Tony Hancock plays a terrible amateur artist who escapes from his dreary city job to find fame as part of the modern art movement in Paris in the 1960s. At a party, he describes the life he left behind to a group of adoring female fans. They all have black turtleneck sweaters, platinum blonde hair, kohl-rimmed eyes and blue lips. Tony Hancock describes London city workers with their identical pinstriped suits, bowler hats, briefcases and umbrellas; his audience of clones murmurs, 'How terrible to be all the same . . .'[2]

As a preparation for prayer, open your eyes to see all those people who do not wear a uniform by choice: the school children, the shop workers, the drivers of delivery vans, the bank clerks. In your prayers, ask God for the will to search out the individual behind the uniform, and the desire to engage with the person, not the corporate packaging.

10 SEPTEMBER

Back to school
Friends

My oldest friends know what I was like when I was in Infant School. They know what clothes and make-up I experimented with in the 1980s, what my first boyfriend was like and what I was told off for by the Head of Sixth Form. We celebrated each other's eighteenth birthdays, went to each other's weddings and became godparents to each other's children. One of them recently sent me a card which read, 'You'll always be my friend. You know too much!'

In a time of quiet, call to mind your oldest friendships. Naming those friends before God, hold and cherish the memory of those experiences you shared, and give thanks for those friendships which last.

11 SEPTEMBER

Back to school
Bullying

> You throw snowballs at enemies and rejoice if they get hit. With enemies you can feel hatred, and anger. But Cordelia is my friend.[3]

These lines come from *Cat's Eye*, a novel which anatomises the complex relationship between two little girls, Cordelia and Elaine, who are friends, but also a bully and her victim. Elaine struggles to understand why her friend often criticises, excludes, mocks and belittles her; being unable to see Cordelia simply as 'an enemy', she concludes that this treatment must be part of the friendship and that she in some way deserves it. The bullying not only wounds her physically and emotionally, it permanently undermines her self-esteem.

In your prayers today, remember all those who are the victims of bullying:

> the child who can't ignore being ignored,
> who longs to be included,
> who wishes they would all stop laughing;
>
> the teenager who feels she can never
>   quite measure up to her parents'

continued overleaf

expectations;

the butt of everyone's jokes at the office;

those who feel they are alone in being bullied by their boss,

and all those who are attacked in the street, in the playground or in their own home by those who want to terrorise and dominate them.

Pray for all those known to you who are bullied.

12 SEPTEMBER

Back to school
Playing

> 'I hate school – it's *completely boring!*'
> 'Well,' I replied brightly to my grumpy child, 'it can't be all bad – there must be something you enjoy.'
> 'Only playtime.'

I used to love playtime (even the word sounds lovely – so much more inviting than 'break'). I still remember the chants, skipping rhymes and elaborate games we invented.

I just wish that I had taken to heart the lesson that the school day teaches, that hard work should be followed by play.

In a time of quiet, consider whether your life has that balance of work and relaxation that God himself ordained when he created the world. Rest in God's presence and pray for the wisdom to see when and how to play, trusting in the transforming power of recreation.

13 SEPTEMBER

Inspirational encounters
The creative spirit

When I met her, Phoebe was in her eighties, living alone in quiet retirement in Kent. She had taught art at the local boarding school, and was herself a talented painter. She was a member of the Royal Miniaturists' Society, and showed me the tiny, beautifully detailed portraits she had exhibited. However, her eyesight was failing, and she could no longer paint miniatures. She had responded by developing a whole new style: she now painted in bold, abstract colours which blurred and spread into one another, like exotic corals on a reef. Her living room was filled with these new paintings. Some looked like caves, full of crystals and shining pools. Others looked like the heart of an ancient wood, with tangled branches and tree trunks furred with moss. They were all vibrant and alive, like her, and it was this spirit in her that inspired me.

In a time of quiet, reflect on those times when you have experienced or encountered such creative energy. Give thanks to God for his animating Spirit, and open your mind and heart to meet him again.

14 SEPTEMBER

Hope

In the room next to my son's on the children's surgical ward, there was a new arrival. She was a high-spirited, profoundly disabled girl, who needed an operation to enable her to receive food directly into her stomach, because she had a very weak swallowing reflex. Her mum chatted and laughed with her, responding to every facial expression her daughter made. When she and I talked over a cup of tea in the hospital canteen, she couldn't speak highly enough of the hospital and the surgeon who was going to make her daughter's life, and her own, so much easier. Her daughter was never going to be 'better', but the operation would allow her to eat without choking, and this was wonderful.

I never found out her name, but this woman showed me that real hope is not insubstantial wishfulness: her hope for her daughter was realistic, dynamic and full of joy. In your prayers today, bring before God all those known to you who need this kind of hope. Pray that a strong and certain hope may sustain them when there seems to be nothing else to hold on to.

15 SEPTEMBER

The still centre

The Franciscan friar was tubby and heartily friendly. He had preached at church that morning and had been invited to the vicarage for lunch, as had I and a couple of college friends. I had never met a member of a religious order before, and was intrigued by his stories of living as a poor, travelling friar who moved around the country for free by hitching lifts. He had had some entertaining rides with people who were understandably curious about a jolly, hitchhiking, habit-wearing monk. After lunch, we went to sit in the vicar's lounge and the family's mad black Labrador cavorted excitedly around, jumping on all the guests. Then the friar reached out his hand and the dog came straight to him. He stroked its head, and the dog was suddenly calm – strikingly so, as it then lay down at his feet and remained there for the rest of the afternoon.

I would like to think that the friar had inherited St Francis' special gift with animals; it seems more likely that the dog responded instinctively to a deep calmness in the man, an inner peace which lay beyond his sociable exterior but could be sensed through it. In your prayers today, reflect on the power of such peace. Consider whether you have encountered it or experienced it, and bring those recollections before God. Rest in his presence as you seek your own still centre.

16 SEPTEMBER
Inspiration

I have always been interested in accounts of artistic inspiration. Sue Townsend, author of the Adrian Mole stories, has said – with some embarrassment – that one day she heard his voice in her head. J. K. Rowling has spoken of how Harry Potter appeared, fully formed, in her mind during a long train journey. I have heard a poet describe himself merely as a conduit for the poetry which flowed into him from somewhere else. Michelangelo is said to have carved his David from a solid block of marble in the belief that the body was already there, and only required his skill to uncover it.

What all these stories share is a sense of the otherness of inspiration: it comes, often unbidden, from outside yourself. From a Christian perspective, inspiration is a moment of encounter and recognition, in which the Holy Spirit is active. The word *inspire* literally means 'to breathe into', deriving from the Latin word *spiritus*, which means both 'breathing' and 'spirit'. In a time of quiet, pray for the Holy Spirit's inspiration:

> Inspiring Spirit,
> fire my imagination
> and kindle my bright ideas;
> Encountering Spirit,
> prompt my hands to reach out
> and my heart to love;
> Provocative Spirit,
> animate and incite me to do your work,
> in the name of the Father, the Son
> and the Holy Spirit.
> Amen.

17 SEPTEMBER

'The Vision of the Cross'
The Warrior-Christ

This Anglo-Saxon poem appears in a book which was probably carried by a cleric on a pilgrimage to Rome about a thousand years ago. It is a dream-vision, in which the Cross itself retells its memories of the Crucifixion:

> The young hero, almighty God, stripped off as if he were going into battle, all bold and resolute. He didn't flinch once as he flung out his strong arms to embrace me, the tall gallows . . . I was raised up as a cross, and – not daring to fall – I held up the mighty King, Heaven's Lord, who was fighting to save humankind.[4]

How startling for us, who are used to images of the patient, suffering Christ, to find him described here as a warrior-hero, battling for our salvation. For our sword-wielding ancestors, this characterisation must have made the Christian God seem more familiar, whereas we tend to think of him as 'nice' – loving, turning the other cheek, passively accepting his fate with perfect faith.

In a time of quiet, look again at the Gospel stories for evidence of the active, angry and forceful Christ.[5] They show him confronting the religious authorities, challenging religious laws, reacting with anger, cursing a harmless tree and rampaging through the market stalls in the temple. For us, a warrior-Christ may be Christ the rebel, the activist, the stirrer. Read and reflect on what his example may mean for us.

18 SEPTEMBER

'The Seafarer'
The lone flier calls...

In this poem from the Dark Ages, the voice we hear is that of an experienced sailor who has no illusions about the harshness of life at sea. He recalls the loneliness, the bone-biting cold, the dangers of rocks and wild waves – and yet he feels irresistibly called to the ocean:

> The thoughts of my heart are urging me now to explore those high tides, that salt surge... He who steers his course towards the waves always has that longing... My heart flies from my breast, my spirit turns seawards and heads across the surface of the earth towards the whale's territory, coming back to me ravenous; the lone flier is calling, irresistibly enticing my heart to follow the whale's path across the ocean's expanse.[6]

When I read this, I think of what it is like to be called – to faith, or to a particular vocation – and how it feels to wrestle with that call. Whether it is finding God, or true love, or a call to ministry, or a feeling that, 'I've just *got* to do this,' there is always that irresistible, urging call which draws you on. Often we are unwilling, or scared, or reluctant, like the Seafarer; sometimes we are joyful and relieved to have made a decision which just feels *right*.

In your prayers, listen for that call. Think back to when you have heard it before: times in your life when you felt drawn to make a particular choice, and made it with peaceful certainty, or in spite of your own reluctance and trepidation. Open your heart, and listen.

Aelfric's *Lives of Saints*
Counting blessings

This volume of homilies, translated into Old English from Latin to be read to monks on saints' days, contains some unexpected gems. One of my favourites is the story of St Swithhun, a dead but very active saint whose bones healed people so prolifically that before long the Anglo-Saxon equivalent of coach parties were bringing the sick to the minster where he was buried. The local bishop ordered the monks there to sing hymns of praise every time a sick person was healed. They began enthusiastically enough, but when the miracles continued round the clock they began to cut down on the singing, reasoning that the bishop was busy with the king and would never know. However, St Swithhun himself appeared to the bishop in a vision and told him the monks were slacking off – threatening, moreover, to stop the healing altogether unless proper praises were sung. The monks, threatened in turn by the bishop with seven days' compulsory fasting, did as they were told, and dutifully praised the continuing miracles.[7]

I love those grumpy monks: they are so human. Surrounded by wonder, they take miracles for granted and giving thanks becomes a chore. I can imagine them grumbling about their zealous saint who goes telling tales to the bishop.

In your prayers today, give thanks for all the blessings you take for granted, and those which you remember daily. If you have some beads, thread them on a string to help you literally count your blessings; keep the threaded beads as a visible reminder of how much you have been given.

20 SEPTEMBER

Sir Gawain and the Green Knight
Lead us not into temptation...

In this long fourteenth-century poem, Sir Gawain faces a terrifying challenge: he must face the unearthly Green Knight and, without defending himself, endure a single blow from a huge axe. Staying at a nearby castle, he unexpectedly faces a different kind of challenge. His host's wife attempts to seduce him on three successive mornings while her husband is out hunting. She playfully demands kisses and then a gift as a love-token. Gawain has nothing to give that is worthy of her, and refuses the valuable ring she offers him. Finally she presses him to accept her green silk belt, claiming it has the power to protect him from harm. At last, Gawain gives in to temptation, and takes the love-token which he believes will enable him to cheat death by the Green Knight's axe.

This medieval poem[8] offers a master-class in temptation. It starts when we are off-guard – Gawain is still asleep – and it works on us by degrees: a kiss seems harmless enough, but having agreed to the first, he can hardly refuse the next two kisses, and then three. The tempter is an expert haggler: having refused the first gift, Gawain has been manoeuvred into accepting her second, cheaper offer. Finally, temptation plays on our deepest vulnerabilities: Gawain's desire to save his skin is the clincher here.

In a time of quiet, reflect on your own experience of being led, by degrees, to accept something you know to be wrong. Perhaps you may recognise the workings of temptation in your life at the moment. Examine those niggling feelings of unease and pray: *lead us not into temptation, but deliver us from evil.*

21 SEPTEMBER

Peace one day

> The wolf shall live with the lamb,
> the leopard shall lie down with the kid,
> the calf and the lion and the fatling together,
> and a little child shall lead them.
> ... They will not hurt or destroy
> on all my holy mountain;
> for the earth will be full of the knowledge
>   of the Lord
> as the waters cover the sea.[9]

Today is the UN International Day of Peace, a recent initiative to establish a day on which hostilities across the world will be suspended. It reminds me of Isaiah's vision of a world in which even the animals co-exist in peace.

In your prayers today, pray that the Prince of Peace might open your mind to a vision of peace one day. Imagine a world in which guns and bombs are no longer used, in which land is no longer coveted and people are no longer killed because of the colour of their skin or the name of their religion. Pray that, in whatever way you can, you too may be a peacemaker.

22 SEPTEMBER

War

It is the end of the first day of the Battle of the Somme, and the scattered survivors have lined up for their company's roll call. Many, many names go unanswered:

> Names came pattering into the dusk, bodying out the places of their forebears, the villages and towns where the telegram would be delivered ... dead towns without life or purpose, without the sounds of fathers and their children, without young men at the factories or in the fields, with no husbands for the women, no deep sound of voices in the inns, with the children who would have been born, who would have grown and worked or painted, even governed, left ungenerated in their fathers' shattered flesh that lay in stinking shell-holes in the beet-crop soil.[10]

Such terrible wasting of human life continues today. As a preparation for prayer, watch the news and see the evidence of the wars which are being fought all over the world. In a time of quiet, bring before God all those who are affected by war:

> the soldiers who have died doing their duty and their comrades who fight on;

continued overleaf

the civilians whose lives have been
destroyed or blighted by war;

those who wait for them, in fear and
hope;

those who have been bereaved

and those who wait for news of the
missing.

Pray that they will know the God of Love and Peace
is with them in the midst of pain and conflict.

23 SEPTEMBER

Siege

Between September 1941 and January 1944, the city of Leningrad was under siege. In the course of 900 days, over a million people died from Hitler's regular bombardments, from the cold of exceptionally bitter winters, from disease and starvation. All supply routes were blockaded and people became increasingly desperate for food and firewood: theft became a way of life and there are even reports of people resorting to cannibalism. Extreme privation led to complete social breakdown.

In your prayers today, remember all those who are under siege in our own time:

> those whose lives are squeezed by international sanctions;
>
> those who must observe the checkpoints and curfews of military rule;
>
> those held prisoner in their homes by the threat of bombs or bullets;
>
> those who have been herded into camps, or ghettos, or detention centres,
>
> and all those who find themselves caught up in conflicts not of their own making.

24 SEPTEMBER
Ceasefire

One of the most moving examples of a ceasefire is that which occurred spontaneously along the Western Front on Christmas Day, 1914. British and German troops climbed out of their trenches to meet in no-man's-land. There are stories of young men kicking footballs around, swapping tobacco and sharing souvenirs. The soldiers also used the time to recover their friends' bodies from the mud and give them a proper burial.

This ceasefire never spread beyond a few trenches, but in other conflicts a ceasefire has been the cornerstone of a lasting peace. In your prayers today, pray for that first move towards the end of violence:

> Peace-loving Lord,
> your Spirit hovers over political handshakes,
> ceasefire declarations
> and peace treaties.
> In the world's conflicts,
> and in the troubled relationships
> and turbulent lives known to us,
> may there be a pause.
> May your peace gain a foothold
> and enter in.
> Amen.

25 SEPTEMBER

Seeds

At this time of year, nature is in a hurry to produce her seeds before the leaves drop and the plants die back for the winter. From dandelions to oak trees, seeds everywhere are shaken loose, dropped to the ground, popped from seed-heads or floated on the wind. Each seed carries the potential for new life in the spring. I am reminded of the Millennium Seed Bank Project at Kew, which aims to preserve the world's most precious plants and flowers by storing their seeds for future generations. In neatly catalogued packages, there are hard, brown beans and powdery specks which are rainforests and wild flower meadows in embryo.

As a preparation for prayer today, walk outside and find a seed or two: a poppy-head, a conker, a sunflower seed or a sycamore's 'helicopter'. Use those seeds as a focus for your prayers, reflecting that all life – including us – begins as a tiny seed. Hold those precious germs of life in your hands as you pray, and praise God for the promise which each seed contains.

26 SEPTEMBER
Sunflowers

I loved growing sunflowers as a child, measuring my height against them as the summer progressed and noticing the way they moved their heavy heads throughout the day to follow the sun. When I saw whole fields of sunflowers in the south of France, the effect was even more startling: they looked like a crowd watching a tennis match in very slow motion, with every head following the arc of the sun across the sky.

In a time of quiet, consider the sunflower as a model of faithfulness, always seeking out the sun and turning towards it. Reflect on your own faith, perhaps using these words:

> Loving Lord, Light of the world,
> I confess that I have hidden my face from you;
> I have not looked for you
> and when you have found me,
> I have turned away.
> I have tried to grow without you,
> and bloom by my own efforts.
> Grant me the humility to turn to you,
> the wisdom to follow you
> and the grace to accept your radiant love.
> Amen.

27 SEPTEMBER
Indian summer

At this time of year, we often enjoy a last, late spell of sunshine and clear skies before the storms of autumn. We call it an 'Indian summer', and the same term is used to describe an unexpected calm which can descend at the very end of life. Doctors are familiar with the way a terminally ill patient can seem to rally and improve shortly before death, and many who have watched a loved one die have seen this for themselves.

In a time of quiet, bring before God all those who are dying, and those who love them to the end. Pray that the peace of God may soothe their pain and fear, fill their souls and bring them rest.

28 SEPTEMBER
Dying back

The footpaths and lanes are starting to widen again. Every summer, the ferns uncurl themselves and spread out their fronds, extending the verges and hedges by at least a foot. By now, the ferns are starting to turn brown and die back. Within a month or so it will look as if the earth has sucked them back inside itself to wait for the spring.

In a time of quiet, rest in God's presence as you contemplate earth's cycle of death and rebirth, and our place within it. Thank God for every part of the circle, using this litany of blessing:

> Blessed be the seeding,
> blessed be the showing,
> blessed be the growing,
> blessed be the blooming,
> blessed be the fading,
> blessed be the dying,
> blessed be the rising,
> blessed be the living
> and blessed be the loving,
> which never ends.
> Amen.

29 SEPTEMBER
Empty nests

> There's nothing in the way now,
> ... there's room enough to fly
> and even though, she's spent her whole
>   life waiting,
> it's never easy letting go.[11]

At this time of year, many parents find themselves with a quiet, empty house for the first time in years, as their youngest child leaves home to go to college. The depression and sense of loss this can cause has been called the 'Empty Nest Syndrome', and the words of this song express the mixed feelings of the daughter who is leaving and of the mother who has to let her go.

In your prayers today, remember all those children who are leaving home, and all those parents who are letting go. Pray that they might have the courage and strength to cope with the first few weeks and months of adjustment.

30 SEPTEMBER
Blackberries

> 'Blackberries in October are the Devil's food.'

This folk saying has its basis in biological fact, because by mid-October blackberries are beginning to be spoiled by insect larvae. *Now* is the opportune moment for blackberrying.

This reminds me of two words the ancient Greeks used for time, *kronos* and *kairos*. *Kronos* referred to the chronological time in which we measure our days; *kairos* meant the right time, the divinely appointed time, the opportune moment. Today, offer your time to God and consider your own *kairos* moment. Are you waiting for the right time to say or do something? Bring your concerns to God in prayer and ask that you might recognise that *kairos* time when it comes.

October

1 OCTOBER

Yesterday

I love reading the obituaries and eulogies that are often printed in parish magazines. They celebrate individual histories in all their surprising, moving, eccentric detail. They remind me that there is no such thing as an 'ordinary' life, and every one of us has a past which is a rich storehouse. As a preparation for prayer today, dust off some old photograph albums or find that shoebox full of mementoes; take some time to look through them and appreciate the wealth of your life experience.

In a time of quiet, give thanks to God for all those dearly loved people, places and events which form the intricate tapestry of your past. Soon, All Souls' Day and Remembrance Sunday will see us looking back with sadness; in your prayers today, remember with joy and gratitude.

2 OCTOBER

Tomorrow

'Why can't it be tomorrow *today*?' demanded my small daughter, when a promised treat would not come fast enough. Tomorrow is governed by a very unreliable clock: if we dread it, it races towards us, and if we long for it, the minutes creep by at a snail's pace.

In a time of quiet, pray for everyone whose thoughts are fixed on tomorrow.

Pray for those who fear what tomorrow will bring:

> a first diagnosis;
>
> a judgement in court;
>
> a confrontation at work;
>
> another day of unemployment or loneliness.

Pray for those who have all their hopes pinned on tomorrow:

> the excited child looking forward to her birthday;
>
> the scientist on the verge of a ground-breaking discovery;
>
> the refugee, the prisoner and the homeless person who hope and pray that in some tomorrow there will be a home for them.

Pray for those who suffer in mind, body or spirit and cannot sleep, so that they lose the comforting rhythm of today and tomorrow; and pray for your own tomorrow.

3 OCTOBER

Today

> Praise with elation,
> praise every morning,
> God's recreation
> of the new day.[1]

Today, reflect on the power of a fresh start, a new dawn. However messily yesterday ended, today may bring renewed energy, clarity of mind or simply a fresh approach to an intractable problem.

In a time of quiet, hold your calendar or diary open in front of you and offer up today in prayer. Each day is a gift: rest in the present moment and receive that gift with thankfulness. Pray for God's guidance in the use of your time.

4 OCTOBER
Eternity

There is a story from the seventh century about a king who is visited by a saint and confronted with Christianity for the first time. One of his counsellors describes his people's current view of human life by comparing it to the brief flight of a sparrow through the great hall in winter:

> In the midst there is a comforting fire to warm the hall; outside, the storms of winter rain or snow are raging. This sparrow flies swiftly in through one door of the hall, and out through another. While he is inside, he is safe from the winter storms; but after a few moments of comfort, he vanishes from sight into the wintry world from which he came.[2]

Human life is perceived as a brief period of light and comfort, before and after which there is nothing but empty, inhospitable darkness. The king recognises the God who will fill that terrifying void of eternity with light, presence and love: he decides that he and his people will embrace the new faith.

In a time of quiet, reflect on this story and its image of the timelessness from which we came, and to which we will return. Our daily lives are ruled by the clock, but God's eternal, infinite presence is beyond time, embracing our little yesterdays, todays and tomorrows.

5 OCTOBER

Time Lord

At this time of year, the television schedules start to fill up with the popular shows which draw the biggest audiences. I am a late convert to *Doctor Who*, and the following prayers are inspired by this example of popular storytelling at its fantastical best.

The Doctor is one of the last Time Lords. Each Time Lord chooses his own name: the Doctor comes to help and heal, while his nemesis, bent on world domination, calls himself the Master. The Doctor is a lonely traveller: he has no home and no family, although on his endless journeying through time and space he often has a companion. He never dies, but regenerates, remaining the same Doctor but with a different face.

Today, take what is Christ-like in this fictional hero and consider it in prayer:

> Lord of all time and matter,
> you are the living Word,
> the Verb of all being and doing.
> Help me know your different faces
> and greet you in friends and strangers,
> in the homeless, the lonely
> and the unloved.
> Show me how to help and make whole,
> and give me the grace to meet this
>   broken world with outstretched arms,
> as you did.
> Amen.

6 OCTOBER
TARDIS

The Doctor's ship is the TARDIS, which stands for Time And Relative Dimension In Space. It is famously much bigger on the inside than it is on the outside: its exterior looks and feels like a 1950s police telephone box, while inside it is a ship built for travel across time and space, containing 'an entire world of time energy within its walls'.[3]

In the Middle Ages, choosing a life of prayer in a monastery was sometimes referred to as 'stepping out of time'. Inside that place of encounter we call prayer, time is indeed different, because we leave behind the ticking clock which rules our everyday lives and look towards God who embraces all time in his eternal present. As a preparation for prayer today, choose a place to pray. Whether it is a room, a quiet corner or a pew, try to envisage it as a place where time is different. This is your praying place: step inside it, out of time and towards the eternal. Be still in God's timeless presence.

7 OCTOBER
Time travel

> Two roads diverged in a wood, and I –
> I took the one less travelled by,
> and that has made all the difference.[4]

Of all the wish-fulfilment fantasies which science fiction explores, time travel is perhaps the best. How different our lives would be if we could go back to undo our mistakes or make different choices, and if we could go forward to discover where we are heading.

In a time of quiet, name before God those actions and choices in your past that you would change if you could. Reflect on what difference they made to your life, and perhaps the lives of others. Confess those irrevocable decisions and pray for the wisdom to learn from them in the future.

8 OCTOBER
Space travel

It is no wonder that outer space has excited our imaginations and spirit of adventure. It is the last great undiscovered country, so vast that there is scope in it for our wildest dreams and imaginings.

In your prayers today, look up into the night sky and feel the presence of the ancient, unknowable reaches of space all around you. It is an abyss so deep and wide that the light of dead stars has yet to reach us. As you become aware of your own littleness, reflect on Paul's words:

> For I am convinced that neither death, nor life, nor angels, nor rulers, nor things present, nor things to come, nor powers, nor height, nor depth, nor anything else in all creation, will be able to separate us from the love of God in Christ Jesus our Lord.[5]

Rest in the presence of the One whose love embraces all time and space.

9 OCTOBER
Priorities

I have always remembered a school assembly in which our head teacher talked about the need to distinguish, in our daily lives, between what is urgent and what is important, and to choose what is most deserving of our attention accordingly. It is a great lesson, but a hard one to follow...

Urgent and important

Some things in our lives demand attention immediately, and it is right that they should do so: a crying child; a friend on the doorstep in tears; raw human need in the aftermath of a hurricane or an earthquake.

In your prayers, bring to mind all those people and situations in need of immediate help:

> the suddenly bereaved;
>
> those made homeless by a disaster;
>
> those known to us who have reached a moment of crisis.

Pray for Christ to step into that darkness which human help alone cannot penetrate.

Pray for yourself or your loved ones, and pray for those whose pain is known only to God.

10 OCTOBER

Urgent but not important

> Now as they went on their way, he entered a certain village, where a woman named Martha welcomed him into her home. She had a sister named Mary, who sat at the Lord's feet and listened to what he was saying. But Martha was distracted by her many tasks; so she came to him and asked, 'Lord, do you not care that my sister has left me to do all the work by myself? Tell her then to help me.' But the Lord answered her, 'Martha, Martha, you are worried and distracted by many things; there is need of only one thing. Mary has chosen the better part, which will not be taken away from her.'[6]

Poor Martha. Anyone who has entertained guests will sympathise with her workload and her desire to be a good hostess. But reflect today on her story and what it tells us about our own lives. How often do we fill our time with chores, just because they are there and are the most immediately obvious things that need doing?

Today, collect together in prayer the many mundane tasks which absorb your time and energy. Lay before God all the busyness which worries and distracts you, and pray that he might show you what 'the better part' is, and how to choose it. Confess the Martha side of you, and seek the Mary side.

11 OCTOBER

Not urgent but important

This is the area which is easiest and most damaging to overlook, because it concerns those things which are such a fundamental part of our lives that we cease thinking about them at all. We simply take them for granted – until a crisis makes them an urgent matter. Think of the long marriage which founders over an affair; the family torn apart by arguments over a will; the prayer life which, like a neglected plant, withers and dies in harsh conditions.

In a time of quiet, reflect on those parts of your life which you could not do without. Give thanks, and pray for the wisdom to perceive how you might tend and cherish these essentials.

12 OCTOBER

Weighing up

Today, try an active form of prayer. Find a large or heavy object that you can hold in your hand, such as an orange or a paperweight, and a small, light object such as a grape or a ball of cotton wool. Hold one object in each open palm, using your hands like a set of scales. Feel the weight of one and the lightness of the other, and pray:

> Lord of wisdom and insight,
> help me to see my life with your eyes.
> Help me to weigh up what is most important
> and what is least important.
> Help me to balance my days
> so that I use my time and energy wisely.
> Help me to remember, in each situation,
> the different weights I hold in my hands now:
> the heavy and the lightweight –
> the vital and the trivial.
> Lord, grant me discernment and the strength
>   to do what is right.
> I ask this in Jesus' name.
> Amen.

13 OCTOBER

The hunt
'The Hound of Heaven'

> I fled him, down the nights and down the days;
> I fled him, down the arches of the years;
> I fled him, down the labyrinthine ways
> of my own mind; and in the mist of tears
> I hid from him, and under running laughter.[7]

When I was a teenager I felt strongly drawn to God, but I resisted taking any formal step towards belonging to a church or even calling myself a Christian, because I was frightened. My early experience of religion had been in school R E lessons, where the most popular method of instruction at that time was the 'true life' examples of people coming to faith through adversity. The stories scared me stiff: young people dying of cancer found God; teenagers maimed by accidents discovered the true meaning of life. In my young mind, becoming a Christian was inextricably linked with very bad things happening to you, and although I understood where my fear came from, I couldn't shake it off. For years I resisted embracing my faith.

In your prayer time, reflect on this poem's description of running away from God and consider whether there are ways in which you have tried to escape him in the past.

Are there still some parts of your life which you try to keep away from him?

Do you sometimes feel like running away from your faith and everything it demands of you?

14 OCTOBER

The pursuit
The Runaway Bunny

In this lovely children's story, a little bunny declares he will run away from his mother. First he says he will turn into a fish to escape from her; his mother replies that in that case, she will turn into a fisherman and catch him. Every escape the little bunny proposes is matched by his mother: whether he becomes a rock on the mountain, a hidden crocus, a bird or a trapeze artist, she will transform herself to find her child wherever he goes, until the little bunny gives in:

> 'Shucks,' said the bunny, 'I might just as well stay where I am and be your little bunny.'
>
> And so he did.
>
> 'Have a carrot,' said the mother bunny.[8]

I have always been moved by this tale of a love so active and adaptable that it will never give up. In your prayer time, consider this story as a parable of Christ's love for us, reflecting on those times you have been conscious of his presence in your life, no matter what strange twists and turns your path may have taken. Consider the simple, loving acceptance which greets the runaway when he finally stops running.

15 OCTOBER

Sought

O Lord, you have searched me
and known me.
You know when I sit down
and when I rise up;
you discern my thoughts from far away ...
You hem me in, behind and before,
and lay your hand upon me.
Such knowledge is too wonderful for me;
it is so high that I cannot attain it.
Where can I go from your spirit?
Or where can I flee from your presence? ...
If I take the wings of the morning
and settle at the farthest limits of the sea,
even there your hand shall lead me,
and your right hand shall hold me fast.[9]

In a time of quiet, reflect on these words from Psalm 139. Whether they make you feel pursued and captured or sought after and loved, let God speak to you through them as you rest in his presence.

16 OCTOBER
Scent

My first job every morning is to let the dog out into the back garden. I am fascinated by the way she uses her nose: to me, the lawn just looks green and ordinary, but her nose can detect the invisible tracks of every hedgehog, mouse or rabbit which crossed it during the night, and she busily follows them all.

In your prayers today, bring before God all those who are trying to find their path in life, and pray that he who is the Way might show them the right track to follow:

> remember especially those who are leaving school;
> those considering a career change;
> those facing a critical decision;
> those listening for their true calling,
> and those who simply don't know what to do.

Pray too for your own journey.

17 OCTOBER

Sabotage

One of the most straightforward ways in which saboteurs disrupt a fox hunt is by using smell. The hounds follow the fox's scent, so the saboteurs use perfume and other strong smells to hide the track and confuse the hounds.

In your prayers today, call to mind those things which make you lose track of God. Confess the little things which get in the way of your attempts to pray; confess the big things which distract you from God or lead you in the wrong direction entirely. Ask for forgiveness and pray for the grace to find your godward path again.

18 OCTOBER
Football

The season of winter sport is in full swing, and once again I am surrounded by football fanatics in our house. If they are not at Plymouth Argyle's Home Park, then they are watching the progress of their rivals on Sky Sports. The following prayers have been inspired by an outsider's view of the 'Beautiful Game'.

Passion

> Some people believe football is a matter of life and death. I'm very disappointed with that attitude. I can assure you it is much, much more important than that.

These words have been attributed to the former Liverpool manager, Bill Shankly, and although their authenticity is in doubt, they are often quoted to show the passion which fans feel for the game. More telling, perhaps, is something Bill Shankly did say: finding a policeman screwing up a Liverpool fan's scarf in his hands, he told him, 'Don't do that. That's somebody's life.'

In a time of quiet, bring before God your own passions. Thank God for those things which have been a part of you for so long that they are a defining part of your life. Pray that through your particular passion you might know yourself better, and see more clearly the fiercely loving God who is at work in the world.

19 OCTOBER
Community

In the black and white photographs of football crowds in the 1930s, the terraces are packed with flat-capped, bowler-hatted and trilby-wearing men, standing cheek by jowl to cheer on their team. On a Saturday afternoon when Plymouth Argyle are at home, the roads leading to Home Park are full of nose-to-tail traffic while on the pavements a steady stream of fans in green and white flows past. Football began in the community, with local fans supporting local teams, and in spite of the high-finance glitz and international glamour of the Premiership, that is where its heart remains. It is a focus for people's sense of identity: they go as pensioners to the ground they first saw as children, and they measure out their lives, Saturday by Saturday, in the successes and failures of their team. At a local football ground, you see a defiant response to the claim, 'There is no such thing as society.'[10] These fans are individuals, some in silly hats, others with face paint and flags, but in supporting their team they share a common passion and purpose.

In a time of quiet, consider your own community. What is it that unites it? In your prayers, bring before God the scattered individuals who make up your community and ask, what might they share? What more could be done to bring people together?

20 OCTOBER

Loyalty

The pensioners who support the local football team have seen every component of their club change many times over the years. Players come and go; managers are hired and fired; boards, directors and even grounds change, but the club remains the same and retains the loyalty of its fans.

I am struck by the example this sets us: football fans demonstrate loyalty to something greater than themselves and the individuals who represent it. All too often, a person's faith in God can be undermined by an encounter with a flawed representative, such as an unsympathetic vicar, a bigoted church leader or an unkind churchgoer. In your prayers today, bring before God any experiences like these which you may have had, and hand them over to him in prayer. Ask for help to look beyond those off-putting people and difficult situations, to seek him who is greater than all.

21 OCTOBER
Failure

> I was a loser. I'd failed. Relegated. Simple as that.[11]

In 1998, in the closing minutes of the season's final game, Plymouth Argyle's Paul Wotton missed an opportunity to score and the team not only lost the match, but were relegated as a result. Photographs show the young man in tears, the hopes of his club and its fans destroyed.

In your prayers today, bring before God all those who feel they have failed:

> those who have competed and lost;
> those who have been interviewed but not appointed;
> those who have been seen but not chosen;
> those who have found love and lost it;
> those who didn't quite make the grade,
> and all those who feel they are losers,
> today and every day.

Pray that the Lord who came to the losers and the lost might encourage them now and always.

22 OCTOBER
Success

'We've only gone and done it!'[12]

Three seasons later, Wotton captained Argyle to victory as they became Third Division champions and were promoted. This time there are photographs of a jubilant team, fists punching the air in triumph as they raise the Championship trophy.

In your prayers today, give thanks for the successes enjoyed by you and those close to you. Whether they are public triumphs or private achievements, hold the joy they brought you in prayer and celebrate, perhaps using these words:

> Let the heart thump,
> let the adrenaline surge,
> let the cheers ring out,
> let the tears run,
> let the word spread.
> Joy be ours in success,
> hope be ours in failure,
> and glory be to the Father,
> glory be to the Son and
> glory be to the Spirit.
> Amen.

23 OCTOBER

Monsters

Just as we explore what it means to be good through our heroes, monsters give a shape to our deepest fears. We tell stories about them as a way of handling those fears safely, containing their power in fictional form. As this week ends with Hallowe'en, the following prayers have been inspired by monsters from popular tales, both ancient and modern.

Hydra

The Hydra was a nine-headed snake monster with poisonous breath which the Greek hero, Heracles, was told to kill. However, every time he cut off one of the heads, more grew in its place.

Sometimes it feels as if the minute we deal with one problem, two more spring up to replace it. In particular, financial difficulties and relationship problems can seem unconquerable. In a time of quiet, bring before God any Hydra-like difficulties facing you or those close to you. Pray for the courage not to be overwhelmed, the strength to persevere and the faith to know that God is at your side as you struggle.

24 OCTOBER
Chimera

The Chimera is a fire-breathing monster from Greek mythology which was made up of different body parts: it had the head of a lion, the body of a goat and a snake's tail. Its shadow stalks many current debates about genetic engineering and embryology research, as does that of a modern chimera, Frankenstein's monster. Parliament recently debated stem cell research and the creation of hybrid embryos, in which an animal egg has its nucleus removed and replaced with human genetic material. Conservative MP Edward Leigh quoted Mary Shelley's nightmare creature:

> If an embryo could talk, perhaps it would echo what Mary Shelley did say in *Frankenstein*: 'I, the miserable and the abandoned, an abortion to be spurned out and kicked and trampled on.'[13]

In your prayers today, whatever your own feelings about this controversial topic, remember before God those who are most closely affected by it:

> those afflicted with diseases for which stem cell research offers the best hope of a cure;
>
> the families who are with them in their suffering;
>
> the doctors who treat them;
> the scientists working in research

continued overleaf

laboratories under pressure of time,
   funding and public opinion;
the lawmakers trying to decide what
   is right,
and all those who wrestle daily with the
   ethics of healing.

25 OCTOBER

Dragon

> Fire leaped from the dragon's jaws. He circled for a while high in the air above them lighting all the lake; the trees by the shores shone like copper and like blood with leaping shadows of dense black at their feet. Then down he swooped straight through the arrow-storm, reckless in his rage, taking no heed to turn his scaly sides towards his foes, seeking only to set their town ablaze.[14]

The dragon in Western folklore was the original weapon of mass destruction. As a byword for danger, it appears on early maps in the famous phrase, 'Here be dragons', used to warn the traveller of unknown and uncharted territory.

In your prayers today, bring before God all those who are standing on the brink of the unknown, apprehensive about what they might find ahead of them:

> the soldiers in enemy territory;
>
> the scientific researchers in hostile lands;
>
> those facing radical surgery or aggressive treatment;
>
> those facing death;
>
> those whose lives are about to be transformed by the breakdown of a relationship,
> by sudden unemployment,
> or by the fearful joy of parenthood.

Pray for all of us as we step into the unknowable future.

26 OCTOBER

Dementors

> And then the thing beneath the hood, whatever it was, drew a long, slow, rattling breath, as though it was trying to suck something more than air from its surroundings.
>
> An intense cold swept over them all . . . It was inside his chest, it was inside his very heart . . .[15]

In the Harry Potter stories, the hideous, hooded Dementors feed on everything joyful and positive; they make you feel as if you will never be happy again. J. K. Rowling has said that they were partly inspired by her experience of depression, and the resemblance is very clear. The approach of a Dementor brings darkness and intense cold. It freezes you, sapping your energy and will. Its influence forces you to relive all the worst moments of your life and to see no hope in the future.

In your prayers today, remember all those known to you who are suffering from depression. Pray for them as they cope with the illness itself and those who misunderstand it: the employer who thinks they are 'not really ill', the friend who thinks they should 'just snap out of it'. Pray too for those who live with a depressed person, who feel every day the impact of the disease.

27 OCTOBER
Cybermen

Old enemies of Doctor Who, the Cybermen have a human brain and nervous system wired within a powerful metal body. These intelligent killing machines are subject to 'emotion inhibitors' which enable them to act without empathy or remorse; however, when these inhibitors were turned off in a recent episode, they were completely incapacitated, driven mad by the emotional impact of what they had done.

These monsters are frightening not because they are completely alien, but because they are too like us for comfort. When we become disengaged from our emotions, it is a sign that something is very wrong. It may be a symptom of depression, trauma, nervous breakdown or mental illness. In your prayers today, bring before God all those who find they cannot feel things as they should. Pray for their healing in body, mind and spirit, and pray for their loved ones who are frightened and hurt by such emotional detachment.

28 OCTOBER

Weeping Angel

One touch from this terrifying creature sends you back into the past. For good. You live out your life and die there, and all the life you would have lived in the present and future is lost. *Doctor Who's* Weeping Angels feed on potentiality, on the energy which would have gone into that life.

In your prayers today, remember before God all those who mourn the loss of a life unlived:

> those whose children have not been conceived;
>
> those who have miscarried or had stillborn babies;
>
> those whose children have died;
>
> those who face their own premature death;
>
> all those who have been bereaved,
>
> and all those who feel that death has robbed them of a future.

29 OCTOBER

Ghost

In the film, *Truly, Madly, Deeply*, a woman's grief over the sudden death of her lover is so fierce that it brings him back from the dead – a ghost, but as real, solid and argumentative as ever. He inhabits her house and shares her bed again. Over the following weeks, they joke and argue together and reminisce about falling in love. He physically stays until their relationship fades naturally to wistful fondness and she starts to fall in love with someone new. His presence and absence chart for us one woman's journey from grief and despair to acceptance of loss and renewed hope.

This film reflects something of the reality of bereavement. You don't 'get over it' in the sense of reaching a point when that loss is no longer part of your life; neither is the loss diminished by time. Rather, the loss remains the same but it becomes part of you, you live with it, and gradually your life grows bigger around it.

Today, pray for all those known to you who are living with bereavement:

> Loving Lord, remember... (*name them*).
> Grief has caught them in its eclipse.
> Be with them in the darkness,
> be with them as the light returns,
> be with them in the full glare
>   of everyday living
> when grief still casts its shadow.
> Amen.

30 OCTOBER

Witch

Witches were thought to cause harm by 'ill-wishing'; in Cornwall, you still hear someone who is a bit off-colour described as looking 'wisht', short for 'ill-wished'.[16]

In the days before bacteria, blight or viruses were properly understood, let alone treated, it must have been a kind of comfort to attribute anything from measles to crop failure to the malign influence of a particular person. By making the witch a scapegoat, people could feel as if they were taking some control over the random misfortunes of life.

In a time of quiet, reflect on the people we use as scapegoats today. Whether it is the hooded youths who have come to epitomise anti-social behaviour, or the teenage mothers who are blamed for social breakdown, consider who tends to be held responsible for the brokenness of our society. Bring before God your own scapegoats; pray that, by confessing your own 'blind spots', you might know yourself better and see more clearly.

31 OCTOBER

Hallowe'en

> From ghoulies and ghosties and long-
> leggety beasties
> and things that go bump in the night,
> Good Lord, deliver us![17]

Behind the orgy of spooky merchandise that is modern Hallowe'en lies the ancient Celtic tradition reflected in this Cornish saying. 31 October was the last day of the Celtic year, a time when the veil between life and death was believed to be at its thinnest, and the souls of the dead could enter this world. Heralding the shortest, darkest days of the year, Hallowe'en was well placed to become a focus for our primal fears of darkness, death and the unknown.

In your prayers today, bring your own fears before God and leave them in his hands:

> Ever-living Father,
> you hold me and know me.
>
> Ever-loving Son,
> your love is stronger than death.
>
> Ever-flaming Spirit,
> your blaze conquers darkness.
>
> Surround me with your three-fold power
> now and always.
> Amen.

November

1 NOVEMBER
All Saints

I once heard an artist describing her use of colour. She explained that her whole working day was spent mixing colours for her paintings, and that sometimes, being immersed in subtle shades and muddied blends, she found it hard to hold on to her sense of pure colour. To clarify her vision she would focus on a collection of semiprecious stones she kept for this purpose. As she gazed into the deep, pure colours of the rocks and crystals, she felt her own sense of true colour return.

This is why we need to remember the saints. They are extraordinary and diverse individuals, and some of their stories may inspire us, fire the imagination or strain our credulity, but they are all examples to which we can lift our eyes when we feel confused and grubbied by this messy, subtle, compromising business of living. As a preparation for prayer, find out about the life of a saint, and hold that knowledge in prayer, letting the saint's example speak to you.

2 NOVEMBER

All Souls

> He was . . . my noon, my midnight, my talk,
> my song;
> I thought that love would last for ever:
> I was wrong.[1]

Today is All Souls' Day, a time for remembering those we have lost. This poet gave shape to his grief in words, but sometimes we have no words, and sometimes not even tears will come.

Today, whether you are remembering a recent loss or bereavements from long ago, simply rest in God's presence and light a candle for each loved one. Let those bright flames be your act of remembrance and your prayer.

3 NOVEMBER
Sparklers

If you want to see an expression of pure wonder and awe, look at the face of a small child holding a sparkler at a bonfire party. Heedless of parental fussing about sparks and discarded sticks, he will stand transfixed by that fizzing white light, eyes shining with joy.

Today, let this image kindle your prayer:

> Lord of light,
> open my eyes to see your incandescent
>   Spirit at work in the world:
> as a playful flame amongst friends,
> as a lantern for the stranger,
> as a torch in the darkness,
> as a bright spark in the mind,
> as a high-voltage flash between lovers,
> as a spreading wildfire of love in action.
> Open my eyes that I might see with
>   childlike wonder and awe.
> Amen.

4 NOVEMBER

Rockets

For me, rockets are the best fireworks because they are a perfect combination of noise and visual spectacle: first, that *whoosh* as they tear into the sky, then a breathless pause before the BANG! – and the explosion blossoms into the darkness like a giant chrysanthemum.

Rockets make me think of a kind of praying which has been described as an 'arrow prayer'. This is the urgent, often wordless prayer which we shoot upwards in a moment of crisis or extreme emotion. If it has words, it may say, 'Help!' or, 'What now?' or, 'Thank you!' Today, consider the rocket as a symbol for prayer. You may suddenly need to shoot a prayer upwards, or you may prefer to let your prayer bloom and grow in a time of quiet.

5 NOVEMBER
Guy Fawkes' Night

The hands-on historians wanted to film what would have happened if Guy Fawkes had succeeded in blowing up Parliament in 1605. On a piece of waste ground, they built a wooden replica of the original Houses of Parliament; then they placed life-size cut-outs of the king, lords and members of the government who would have been inside at the time. They replicated the number of barrels of gunpowder which Fawkes had placed in a cellar. The fuse was set and the area was evacuated. With all the excitement of children with a big, noisy toy, the historians pressed the detonator – and instantly the whole structure exploded sky-high. By the time they were able to pick their way through the rubble, their mood had changed. This was a scene of complete devastation and they were shocked. They began to identify pieces of the cut-out figures all over the site, realising that there would have been little of anyone left to bury. There was nothing but a few upright timbers left standing. They were looking at what would have been a seventeenth-century Ground Zero.

In your prayers today, remember all those whose lives have been blown apart by acts of terrorism. Pray for those who have died, for those who mourn them and for those who still bear the mental and physical scars of the attack.

6 NOVEMBER

Bonfires
Pyres

Sometimes a bonfire is a weapon. In the past, people of faith were burnt at the stake for heresy; the Nazis burned books which they believed were 'degenerate', and even today, a person may be burned in effigy as an act of protest.

In your prayers today, remember before God all those who are persecuted for their beliefs, actions or way of life:

> pray for those you believe to be right,
> whose persecutors you condemn;
>
> pray for those you believe to be wrong,
> whose condemnation you endorse.

7 NOVEMBER

Bonfires
Beacons

In the days before instant global communication, an early-warning system was devised to alert England to an attack. On a high hill or tower, a fire would be lit which could be seen from the next highest point across the countryside, where another beacon would be set alight. From cliff top to moorland peak, a chain of fire would spread across the country, calling men to arms. Famously, this system was used to warn of the coming Armada in 1588; since then, it has been an act of celebration, for example on that victory's anniversary in 1988, and again to mark the Millennium.

In your prayers today, hold this image in your mind and let those beacons speak to you of united endeavour and shared hope:

> Lord of all hope,
> may our families, communities and country
> be united by the infectious fire of your Spirit,
> until the world blazes with your love and
>   grace,
> a beacon of hope to all.
> Amen.

8 NOVEMBER

Storytelling

> Today the storytelling begins. Everywhere in Brittany the storytelling begins at Toussaint [All Saints' Day], in the Black Month. It goes on through December, the Very Black Month, as far as the Christmas story.[2]

In this storytelling season, the following suggestions for prayer have been inspired by some of our most enduring and best-loved tales. They are stories which tell us about ourselves.

Cinderella
True love

The basic plot of Cinderella is found in stories all over the world, and underpins many popular romances, from *Pride and Prejudice* to *Pretty Woman*. It is the ultimate tale of romantic wish-fulfilment, in which the humble and overlooked girl finds her true worth recognised and is rewarded with true love, wealth and status.

Cinderella tells us what finding love is like: your beloved chooses you, and you alone, from the crowd. However hard the others try to be Miss or Mr Right, you – just as you are – are the only one who is wanted. In a time of quiet, give thanks for the loved ones in your life who have chosen *you*: the partner or friends to whom you are special because you are you. Remember that this is how God loves you, too: not as a holier, cleverer, wiser version of yourself, but as *you*.

9 NOVEMBER

The Red Shoes
Dangerous temptations

> Sensible footwear
> is just too hard to bear.
> Shoes as red as desire
> that's what I crave.[3]

A girl sees a princess wearing a pair of red shoes, and she longs for them. She lies to get them and defies her blind guardian by wearing them to church. She thinks of nothing else, until the cursed shoes develop a will of their own. They stick fast to her feet and they won't stop dancing, until the exhausted girl persuades an executioner to cut off her feet with the shoes still on them. Humbled, and with wooden feet, she finds redemption.

This brutal tale is the story of addiction: a choice is made which then begins to take over the addict's life, until she becomes controlled by her addiction and the only way to escape it is through radical and painful action. The girl could be today's drug addict or alcoholic; the compulsive shopper whose debts are spiralling out of control; the teenager starving herself to reach size zero; the gambler whose obsession is as tempting and damaging as the red shoes.

In your prayers, reflect on this tale and confess your own 'red shoes'. Bring before God those things in your life which may be starting to control you, and ask for his help in restoring the right balance.

10 NOVEMBER

The Emperor's New Clothes
Truth-telling

Two swindlers claim they have invented a rare and beautiful fabric which is invisible to those who are unfit for their office or very stupid. Fearing for their reputations, the vain emperor and his courtiers deny the evidence of their own eyes and praise the beauty of the 'fabric', which is then made into a new suit for the emperor. As he parades naked through the town, the crowds applaud his new clothes until a small boy declares the truth – and at once the people see the emperor as he really is.

Self-delusion is a powerful thing. Our minds are such complex creations that we can know something in one part of ourselves, while simultaneously believing the opposite. We can mislead others and fool ourselves. However, in this story, the integrity of one small boy who simply tells the truth gives others the courage to tell the truth, too.

In a time of reflection, ask God to open your eyes:

Father God,
let me know the ways in which I am
 fooling myself;
remind me, with your gentle insistence,
 of the truths I already know.
Spirit of Truth,

continued overleaf

show me the reality of those relationships
   and situations which are troubling me.
Brother Christ,
be at my side to encourage me as I try to
   act on my knowledge of the truth.
Amen.

11 NOVEMBER

The Little Mermaid
Choice and sacrifice

The little mermaid falls in love with a human prince and chooses to take on human form so that she can marry her beloved and win for herself an immortal soul. But her heart's desire comes at a price: she is condemned to live in pain, and each step she takes with her new legs will hurt as if she is walking on knives. She must also sacrifice her beautiful and unique voice.

The little mermaid is a girl who knows she can't have it all – but she still makes the choice she knows she must make. In your prayers today, reflect on the life-choices you have made, and the sacrifices they have entailed: choices about relationships, where to live, what job to do, whether to have children and who will care for them. Bring before God the choices you have yet to make and ask for his help in counting the cost of your decision.

12 NOVEMBER
Solomon's justice

The two women stood before Solomon and argued. They had both lost their newborn sons: one baby had died, and the other had been taken to replace him. Both claimed that the living child was their own. Solomon ruled that the baby should be cut in half with a sword and divided equally between the women. This outrageous proposition reveals the true mother, because she willingly renounces her claim rather than see her baby killed. Her child is returned to her, justice is done and Solomon's wisdom is praised.[4]

There is a saying in the legal profession: 'Hard cases make bad law.' The modern practice of law is informed by precedent, so that previous judgements inform current decisions. This means that a difficult and unusual case such as Solomon's would create a strange precedent, namely that cases of disputed parenthood should be resolved by threatening to execute the child in question.

In your prayers today, remember all those faced with difficult decisions, whose judgement will affect other people's lives. Whether they hold public office and their rulings affect us all, or they are individuals trying to make just decisions within the family, ask that they might be blessed with God's wisdom and discernment.

13 NOVEMBER
Thirst for justice

> Blessed are those who hunger and thirst
> for righteousness, for they will be filled.[5]

When I think of someone having this kind of visceral longing for justice, I think of a man called Clive Stafford Smith who is driven to bring justice to the poor and the powerless. He worked for many years to represent prisoners on Death Row in the southern United States; now he is working on behalf of detainees at Guantánamo Bay. His enemies see him as using 'his talents to help very evil people', while one of those he helped at Guantánamo said simply, 'He offered me hope that I would go home. What made a difference was his passion.'[6]

In your prayers today, bring before God all those who long for justice in this world:

> the victims who see crimes go
> unpunished and criminals walk free;
>
> the suspects who are imprisoned
> without trial;
>
> the justly and unjustly accused who are
> denied a fair trial,
>
> and all those who fight injustice
> wherever they find it.

14 NOVEMBER

Mercy

> The kingdom of heaven may be compared to a king who wished to settle accounts with his slaves. When he began the reckoning, one who owed him ten thousand talents was brought to him; and, as he could not pay, his lord ordered him to be sold, together with his wife and children and all his possessions, and payment to be made. So the slave fell on his knees before him, saying, 'Have patience with me, and I will pay you everything.' And out of pity for him, the lord of that slave released him and forgave him the debt.[7]

In your prayers today, reflect on this parable of forgiveness:

> Merciful Lord,
> I owe you everything I have, even my life,
> yet I give you so little in return.
> Forgive me for the times I have repaid
>   my debt in unsaid prayers,
> thoughtless words,
> heedless actions
> and careless inaction;
> have mercy on me,
> not according to my deserving
> but to your faithful, hopeful,
>   enduring love.
> Amen.

15 NOVEMBER
Merciful

> But that same slave, as he went out, came upon one of his fellow-slaves who owed him a hundred denarii; and seizing him by the throat, he said, 'Pay what you owe.' Then his fellow-slave fell down and pleaded with him, 'Have patience with me, and I will pay you.' But he refused; then he went and threw him into prison until he should pay the debt.[8]

As the slave discovers, it is easier to receive mercy than to exercise it yourself. I am reminded of the famous description of mercy:

> The quality of mercy is not strain'd,
> it droppeth as the gentle rain from heaven
> upon the place beneath.[9]

The lawyer who is speaking makes mercy sound easy, as if dropping your claim for something to which you know you are legitimately entitled is as effortless as dropping water from rain clouds. In reality, if you have to give up a legal claim or write off a debt you are owed, it can feel as if forgiveness is being wrung out of you. It is a real effort and you wrestle with it.

In a time of quiet, bring before God all those whom you are struggling to forgive. Confess your sense of injustice, your anger at being wronged and all the other feelings that are fighting against forgiveness; pray for the will and the strength to forgive.

16 NOVEMBER

Prayer directions
Horizontal prayer

When I first started going to church, someone told me to watch out for 'horizontal praying'. This refers to prayers which are not aimed 'upward', to God, but directed straight ahead to the people. These are pointed prayers with an agenda: 'O God, we thank you for our priests and ministers, and pray that *those people* who criticise and complain might understand how hard they work for this church, especially considering the new Church Roof Fund and the PCC which is still looking for a new treasurer...'

In your prayers today, bring before God all those who are so bogged down by worry and trouble that they find it hard to lift their hearts upwards in prayer. Pray for yourself, bringing before God all those things, people and situations that harass you. Lay down those burdens as if you are throwing sandbags out of a hot air balloon, and let your spirit lift towards God in prayer.

17 NOVEMBER

Prayer directions
Upward prayer

In his revolutionary book, *Honest to God*, John Robinson begins by examining the biblical tradition of seeing God and Heaven as 'up there', and the devil and hell as 'down there'. He challenges our often unconscious assumption that, even in this era of space travel and astronomical discovery, God is still, in some way, 'up there' or 'out there'.[10] He then quotes this inspiring passage, in which God is described not as beyond and above us, but as our foundation:

> The name of this infinite and inexhaustible depth and ground of all being is God. That depth is what the word God means. And if that word has not much meaning for you, translate it, and speak of the depths of your life, of the source of your being, of your ultimate concern, of what you take seriously without any reservation.[11]

In a time of quiet, consider where you think of God as being. Reflect on this passage in prayer, letting the words resonate within you.

18 NOVEMBER

Prayer directions
Outward prayer

I have always been interested in body language, and especially in the gestures we all unconsciously use and understand. Picture yourself at a large gathering such as a party or a wedding, where lots of guests are milling around and chatting. You are the host and you want everyone to gather round for photographs or a speech. As you call for people's attention, what gesture do you use to gather everyone in front of you? Most of us would spread our arms out wide, perhaps flapping our hands in a swimming motion to move people together and bring them in.

This very open, 'gathering' gesture is what I associate with 'outward' prayer, which I see as the supplicatory prayers we make in response to the needs of the world around us. God knows all these needs before we name them: we are not introducing them to him for the first time, we are simply gathering together those which are already present and close to our hearts.

In a time of quiet, consider those needs which you want to gather in prayer. Perhaps using the gathering gesture, bring them before God and hold them in his presence.

19 NOVEMBER

Prayer directions
Inward prayer

What tends to happen is this: I sit quietly and close my eyes. I try to regulate my breathing and still myself. I think of 'inward' prayer as being a self-examination, perhaps leading to a prayer of confession, and I try to focus my mind on God and look sternly at my current state. As I go over recent events in my head, the emotions I felt come back to me. If someone made me angry, I find myself revising what I should have said to them – and then I try to focus again. And again. Before I know it, I've drifted into absent-minded navel-gazing. What I need when this happens is a prayer to focus my attention both inwardly and on God.

In a time of quiet today, and whenever you feel distracted in prayer, try saying these words:

> God be in my head,
> and in my understanding;
> God be in my eyes,
> and in my looking;
> God be in my mouth,
> and in my speaking;
> God be in my heart,
> and in my thinking;
> God be at my end,
> and at my departing.[12]

20 NOVEMBER

Prayer directions
Downward prayer

> Living Word, One with the Highest,
> our only Hope,
> heaven and earth's eternal Light,
> we break the silence of this peaceful night:
> Divine Saviour, look down upon us!
> Pour on us the fire of your powerful grace,
> so that all hell might flee at the sound of
>   your voice.[13]

This canticle, written in French, is a lovely example of a prayer which asks for God's Holy Spirit, grace or blessing to come *down* upon us. The word used here for 'pour', *répands*, also means 'spill, scatter, spread out, lavish': we need God's grace not in drips and drops, but in an outpouring which drenches us like a summer storm.

In your prayers today, hold this feeling of need and pray for yourself, and for those whose needs are known to you:

> Divine Saviour, look down upon us;
> pour on us the fire of your powerful grace.
> Amen.

21 NOVEMBER

Prayer directions
Open prayer

I have a book about prayer which has a striking cover. It shows a sculpture by Olivia Sanders called *I It Am*, which is a life-size cement figure standing with a peaceful expression, eyes closed as if in concentration. The middle of the chest is open, cut from collarbone to waist. At heart-height, the figure's hands are held in an open gesture, as if lifting something out or carrying something in.[14]

I often think of this open-hearted figure when I try to pray in a way which is open and receptive. Today, rest in God's presence and be still. Try not to worry about what to say or do. Simply hold your hands open before you, ready to offer and receive.

22 NOVEMBER

The King

In the Church calendar, the last Sunday before Advent celebrates Christ the King. This is the title which encompasses Jesus' life: as a newborn baby, he is visited by the wise men who pay homage to him as the King of the Jews, and it is this name which excites King Herod's murderous interest. At his death, a sign reading, 'Jesus of Nazareth, the King of the Jews', in three languages is nailed above his head on the cross. Even his enemies will not take that name away from him:

> Then the chief priests of the Jews said to Pilate, 'Do not write, "The King of the Jews", but, "This man said, I am King of the Jews."' Pilate answered, 'What I have written I have written.'[15]

Look at the context in which his kingship is spelt out: at first he is a baby, asleep in an animal's feeding trough, whom soldiers have been sent to kill; at the end he is suffering the punishment of a common criminal. And yet he is Christ the King.

In your prayers today, rest in God's presence and reflect on 'our Servant King'.[16] He is Lord of all, and yet he lived a humble life in which he was persecuted and rejected. As the Christmas season approaches, give thanks for the birth of this King among us.

23 NOVEMBER

The baby

The Gospels do not dwell on Jesus' childhood. Luke has the most to say, but even he skips from when Jesus was twelve to when he began his ministry at around thirty. We never hear about Jesus the toddler, the growing boy, the teenager. However, there is one word which connects us with his infancy, and that is the word we translate as 'Father'. When the disciples ask Jesus how to pray, he teaches them the Lord's Prayer. Where we begin, 'Our Father', Jesus used the word *Abba*, which means 'Daddy'. This is one of those very first words which a baby can form with his mouth, like 'mama' and 'dada'. *Abba*: this is how Jesus, as an adult, related to God, and how he taught his disciples – and us – to relate to him. The Lord's Prayer is a simple prayer of intimate, loving connection.

In your prayers today, try saying through the Lord's Prayer in the form you know best, or in Luke's version:

> Daddy,
> *hallowed be your name.*
> *Your kingdom come.*
> *Give us each day our daily bread.*
> *And forgive us our sins,*
> *for we ourselves forgive everyone indebted to us.*
> *And do not bring us to the time of trial.*[17]
> Amen.

24 NOVEMBER

The good shepherd

I was listening to a man who had spent much of his long life raising sheep, as he told me about looking after newborn lambs. He would bring those that were suffering from hypothermia into the house and tuck them up in a box on top of the Aga. The worst cases could appear dead, and he put these inside the oven itself, leaving the door open, to warm them back to life. Rejected lambs or those born as triplets or quads might need hand-feeding, with a bottle, every four hours, but it could be just as labour-intensive to persuade a ewe to foster a lamb which was not her own. This required hands-on intervention, including covering the lamb with all the juices and smells of birth to encourage the parental bond to form.

When Jesus said, 'I am the good shepherd,'[18] he was using an image with which his listeners would have been very familiar, and they would have immediately understood the ways in which a shepherd knows his flock and watches over it, caring for each sheep and lamb. Most of us outside farming communities have no such knowledge, but the experiences of this sheep farmer stuck in my mind. I was reminded of the words of the Lord in Ezekiel: 'I will seek the lost, and I will bring back the strayed, and I will bind up the injured, and I will strengthen the weak.'[19]

In your prayers today, remember before God all those known to you who particularly need this kind of tender, healing care from the Good Shepherd. Pray for yourself, and pray for all those who are lost, unloved, rejected, broken and weak.

25 NOVEMBER

The Word

> In the beginning was the Word, and the Word was with God, and the Word was God. He was in the beginning with God. All things came into being through him, and without him not one thing came into being. What has come into being in him was life, and the life was the light of all people.[20]

This famous passage has always intrigued me because I find its meaning hard to grasp. How is Christ 'the Word'? What does that really mean, and why was the Word of such primary importance to the Creation? Then I discovered, quite by chance, that the French translation for 'the Word' is *le Verbe*. A light bulb went on in my head: Jesus is the Verb of God. The verb connects the subject of a sentence with everything that concerns that subject. In the sentence, 'God created the world,' 'created' is the verb, the connection between 'God' and 'the world' which makes the sentence happen. A sentence with no verb has no life, no action and, in fact, does not exist as a sentence at all. It is just a formless, confused collection of words.

Today, take some time to reflect on the passage above from John's Gospel. In your prayers, give thanks for the Verb of God, who brought us into being and into connection with God.

26 NOVEMBER
The Way

> Who am I?
> I'm the course of years,
> the force of life . . .
> I'm not the instant answer
> to your quick request . . .
> I am the Way.[21]

This poem reflects on Christ's words, 'I am the way, and the truth, and the life. No one comes to the Father except through me.'[22] As the Way, he is a route or a pathway for us: not a quick-fix solution, but an ongoing journey. He is with us over the course of a lifetime, an active, dynamic, continuing Presence.

Today, make your prayer an active form of meditation. Just as Christians over the centuries have followed the Way by making a pilgrimage, go on a walk or a journey today and as you do so, let the words, 'I am the Way,' repeat in your mind, and ask God to speak to you through them. As you travel, let your mind open in prayer.

27 NOVEMBER
Light

In the beginning when God created the heavens and the earth, the earth was a formless void and darkness covered the face of the deep, while a wind from God swept over the face of the waters. Then God said, 'Let there be light'; and there was light. And God saw that the light was good; and God separated the light from the darkness.[23]

At this time of year, as the days get shorter and the nights get longer, daylight becomes more and more precious. In your prayers today, give thanks for this essential gift which we tend to take for granted:

Lord of life,
thank you for the light:
for the first thought of creation in the
 void's chaos;
for the first gift of life after the womb's
 warmth.
Thank you for the new light of another day,
for the old light of the sun,
and for your eternal light,
your radiant love.
Amen.

28 NOVEMBER

Dark

The cellar is in complete darkness. The female FBI agent is alone and searching for the murderer she has been hunting. Now she is the one being hunted, because he is armed and in the cellar with her – and he is wearing night vision goggles. We see her from his point of view, in the eerie green light which makes darkness visible to him. She blunders about in terror, eyes wide, breath coming in shallow gasps, hands fumbling for something to hold on to.

This scene, from the climax of *The Silence of the Lambs*, plays very successfully on our fear of the dark. Watching it, we empathise completely with the heroine and her sense of panic, confusion and terror. It reminds me of the kind of darkness which is used by this poet to represent his view of a world without faith:

> ... neither joy, nor love, nor light,
> nor certitude, nor peace, nor help for pain;
> and we are here as on a darkling plain
> swept with confused alarms of struggle
>   and flight,
> where ignorant armies clash by night.[24]

In your prayers today, bring before God those known to you whose lives are overwhelmed by this kind of darkness. Pray for them, pray for yourself, and pray for all those who are struggling in the darkness of fear, confusion and despair.

29 NOVEMBER

Light in the darkness

I recently visited a disused Cornish slate mine. We were taken through narrow corridors deep into the caves. They had been carved out by men and boys who had laboured for twelve hours at a stretch with hand-held tools. In the deepest part of the mine, our guide explained the chisel marks we could see in the well-lit walls, and described the miners' working conditions. To emphasise his point, he turned all the electric lights off. The blackness was absolute: I waited for my eyes to adjust, but they didn't. It felt as if I was trapped and blindfolded, but the strange echoes and stone-cold air reminded me that I was surrounded by the unseen and unknown depths of a very big cave. After a minute, the guide lit a single candle, which was the light by which each miner worked. It was a tiny light, but after all that darkness it looked unbelievably warm and strong.

Remembering those for whom you prayed yesterday, light a candle today for all those who need this kind of light. In a time of quiet, contemplate that light and call to mind Christ's words:

> I am the light of the world. Whoever
> follows me will never walk in darkness
> but will have the light of life.[25]

30 NOVEMBER

Searchlight

A single desk lamp in a dark room shines full in the face of one person, while someone else sits in shadow, behind the light. In any film or TV drama, we immediately understand this visual clue, and know that the person in the light is under interrogation.

In your prayers today, sit in God's presence and turn this forensic light on yourself, using this prayer based on Psalm 139:

> O Lord, you have searched me
>   and known me:
> even before a word is on my tongue
>   you know it completely.
> You know what I am sorry for,
> what I wish I hadn't said and done,
> what I am reluctant to admit,
> and what I am loathe to give up.
> Search out my sins,
> take them and make me whole.
> Amen.

December

1 DECEMBER

Advent calendar

> A voice cries out:
> 'In the wilderness prepare the way of
>   the Lord,
> make straight in the desert a highway
>   for our God.'[1]

As Advent begins, we enter a time of waiting and preparation. The next twenty-four days are the most carefully counted of the year, as doors on Advent calendars are opened one by one, or Advent candles burn down a little more each day. With these actions we empty and consume: doors are unsealed, perhaps chocolate is eaten, wax is burned. It is as if we are gobbling up the days before Christmas.

In a time of quiet, consider how you might mark the progress of Advent by making and preparing something, rather than using it up. If you have a nativity scene, try making a pathway which leads to it, with one small stone for each day. You could adopt a symbolic action devised by the Iona community, in which strips of cloth are laid across a wooden fruit box, as if preparing a simple manger for the Christ child.[2] You could build a 'prayer-cairn' of pebbles or thread beads on a string, with a cross as the last one. Whatever you choose, make that action your simple prayer of preparation throughout Advent.

2 DECEMBER

Fast

> If we had some ham, we could have some
> ham and eggs – if we had any eggs.[3]

Advent is a season of penitence and was once, like Lent, a time for fasting. For our ancestors living off the land, it was in any case a lean and hungry time of year, as the fruits of the harvest had to be eked out to last the winter. These days, the emphasis is on stocking up for the Christmas feast ahead.

Pause and step aside from that general, headlong rush towards feasting: today, offer in prayer the time you would have spent eating a meal. Thank God for the rhythm of feasting and fasting which runs through nature's calendar. Pray for yourself, that your hunger today might be filled with good things; pray too for those who are famished and have no promise of a coming feast.

3 DECEMBER

Feast

> In glass bells and dishes lie the chocolates, the pralines, Venus' nipples, truffles, *mendiants*, candied fruits, hazelnut clusters, chocolate seashells, candied rose-petals, sugared violets . . . they gleam darkly, like sunken treasure, Aladdin's cave of sweet clichés.[4]

This mouth-watering window display is being described by the austere priest in the novel *Chocolat*. He sees the arrival of this *chocolaterie* in his little town during Lent as a wicked, sensual temptation; however, as the story unfolds, it proves to have a liberating, life-affirming influence. Through the sharing of chocolate and, later, the enjoyment of a lavish birthday feast, families are brought together, the unhappy are comforted, friendships forged and social divisions healed.

In your prayers today, as you look forward to Christmas festivities, thank God for the power of feasting to bring people together in love and friendship. Give thanks for the pleasure of hospitality given and received, and for the delightful satisfaction of good food shared.

4 DECEMBER
Nobody

> As I was going up the stair
> I saw a man who wasn't there.
> He wasn't there again today
> I wish, I *wish* he'd stay away.[5]

In your prayers today, bring before God the 'nobodies' in our society, the powerless, voiceless, marginalised people who are often viewed as a problem we wish would simply go away. Pray for the poor, the homeless, the addicts, the illegal immigrants and all those whom society rejects. Pray too for those people closer to home who are often ignored: the cantankerous elderly woman with no one to visit her; the lonely disabled man who has carers but not friends; the shy teenage mum sitting on her own at the mums-and-toddlers group.

5 DECEMBER

No one

> Mister Cellophane
> shoulda been my name...
> 'cause you can look right through me,
> walk right by me
> and never know I'm there...[6]

This lament, sung by a rejected husband, expresses how we can all feel on occasions. I did when an acquaintance came to dinner and then, three months later, entirely failed to recognise me at a meeting. She looked at me blankly until I told her my husband's name. It made me feel as if I was a nobody who only became somebody by association.

In your prayers today, bring before God those times when you may have felt like Mr Cellophane, and perhaps those occasions when you have unwittingly caused someone else to do so. Remember too those who suffer from low self-esteem, who spend their lives feeling this way:

> Lover of the lowliest and the least,
> you know each son and daughter of yours
> who feels like an empty nobody,
> worth nothing and going nowhere.
> May you fill them with the fullness of life
> and love them back to loving themselves.
> Amen.

6 DECEMBER

Somebody

How do we find out who we are? Where do we get our sense of identity? The TV programme, *Who Do You Think You Are?* shows how popular genealogy has become, and suggests that many people find their identity in their family tree. I love Philip Pullman's idea in the trilogy, *His Dark Materials*: his characters have their spirit – their 'daemon' – outside themselves, visible in animal form. Children's daemons can change shape at will, but as the child grows, they take on a fixed form. It is by the form your daemon finally takes that you know who you are.

In a time of quiet, consider how you know who you are. Bring before God all those parts of your life, good and bad, that have helped form your identity: your family background, your life's experiences, your loved ones, your faith, your work, your friends . . . Whatever it is that has made you who you are, and whether you recall it with joy, thankfulness, pain or regret, know that God's love encompasses it all and embraces you, just as you are.

7 DECEMBER
Decorations

From the tinsel round the windows at the bank to the lights suspended above the High Street, Christmas decorations are everywhere, and nothing says 'Christmas cheer' like something twinkly or sparkly on a damp December afternoon. As you unpack your own decorations, safely put away since last Christmas, find your favourite: a bauble from childhood or a glittering star for the tree. Enjoy the colour and the sparkle, and the festive feeling of anticipation it gives you.

In your prayers, reflect that this represents only half of the preparations for Christmas. The decorations are the external aspect, but what about your own, internal preparation for the celebration of Christ's birth? You might follow an Advent reading course, attend a Quiet Day or renew a discipline of regular prayers. Today, consider what you might do; wherever you hang that decoration, use it as a reminder of your spiritual preparation for Christmas.

8 DECEMBER
Shopping

Most of us will soon spend time and money in one of our big supermarkets, where everything is shiny, fresh and inviting. As a preparation for prayer, try looking at the crammed aisles with different eyes: Deluxe Christmas puddings, Value Christmas puddings, Traditional, Nut-Free, Boozy, Low-fat, Christmas puddings for one; mince pies – three boxes for the price of two; Christmas nuts – buy one bag, get one free; special offers on multiple purchases of whisky and sherry; gift boxes of chocolates and biscuits piled on top of the shelves, higher than we can reach.

In a time of quiet, consider how all this would appear to someone from an Indian shanty town, or a famished African country.

Consider the poor of our own country, humiliated and in debt as they struggle to buy Christmas for their families.

Consider the wealth and consumption we take for granted.

In prayer, confess your own temptation to consume, your own need to have more, and repent. Ask for the grace to see your needs in proportion to those of the hungry developing world, and to spend your comparative wealth wisely.

9 DECEMBER
Hospitality

The Christmas period can be a busy one for social events. Many of us make a special effort to offer hospitality to friends and neighbours, and often reach out to include those who are lonely or are on the margins of our society. For the Son of God whose parents found no room at the inn, sharing food and sharing himself in the company of friends became an integral part of his ministry.

In your prayers today, give thanks for friends and for the many kinds of giving and receiving that form these friendships: the support and encouragement given, the practical help accepted, the laughter and confidences shared. Pray with thankfulness, and open your heart to new calls to be a friend.

10 DECEMBER

Presents

> What can I give him,
> poor as I am?
> If I were a shepherd,
> I would bring a lamb;
> If I were a wise man,
> I would do my part;
> yet what I can I give him –
> give my heart.[7]

One Christmas, my sister-in-law spent £1 on each of our presents, and gave the rest of the money she would normally have spent to charity. Although the monetary value of our presents was small, they cost her a lot of time, energy and thoughtfulness, as she scoured the shops for appropriate gifts for each of us within her narrow budget.

Today, reflect on your Christmas giving and what – apart from money – it cost you:

> Lord,
> teach me how to give my heart to others,
> and in so doing, to give it to you.
> Help me to look beyond the gift-wrapped parcels
> to understand the kind of giving which really counts,
> and show me where this is most needed.
> Amen.

11 DECEMBER

Cards

Our mantelpiece is getting full, the top of the piano is bristling and the strings hanging against the wall are starting to sag. Christmas cards – they keep on coming. Although getting them written and posted in time is a mad dash, it is worth it for this tangible evidence that we are still on someone's list, even if we haven't seen each other or spoken in years.

In a time of quiet, use the Christmas cards you have received as a focus for prayer. Gather them together and thank God for all those who have remembered you: those you see regularly, those who only get in touch at Christmas and those you had forgotten. Pray too for those who seldom receive a Christmas card from anyone.

12 DECEMBER

Lists

The countdown to Christmas is nearly over, with only twelve shopping days left and still so much to do. My kitchen noticeboard is a crazy collage of lists: jobs to do, things to cook, food to buy, meat to collect from the butcher, items for the children to take to school, church events. There are carefully considered lists on lined A4 and urgent notes on pink Post-its.

In a time of quiet, hold in prayer whatever represents for you the particular demands of this time of year. It may be a pile of lists, a busy calendar, or a diary which is emptier than you had hoped. Whatever it is, place it in God's hands and ask for his blessing upon you at this time, as you struggle with too much to do, or too much time alone.

13 DECEMBER

Angels

Angels are all around us now: their snowy wings adorn our Christmas cards, their tiny figures sit among the fairy lights and little girls compete for the privilege of wearing a white sheet, a tinsel halo and some cardboard wings in the Nativity play. For me, these heavenly messengers are more believably depicted in the illustrations for a children's book called *Angels, Angels All Around*.[8] In these stories of biblical encounters with angels, the artist shows working angels with homely faces and strong hands. The angel who rescues Daniel in the lions' den has a heavy beard and kind, crinkly eyes. He handles the lions like a man who has spent his life working with big cats, scratching the big male behind his ears, just where he likes it. The angel who releases Peter from prison is a plain, practical-looking woman with a briskly encouraging smile and a key hanging from her stout waist.

In your prayers today, consider the angels and reflect on these manifestations of God's power at work in the world. Recall the stories of angelic help in the Bible,[9] and thank God for these reminders of his intervention in our lives, then and now.

14 DECEMBER
Devils

In popular storytelling, from the medieval mystery plays to the modern film, *Dogma*, the angels' opposite numbers are the devils who serve the Devil himself. Just as angels intervene to help, heal and rescue, so the devils interfere in order to spoil, damage and destroy. This is dramatised in C. S. Lewis' *The Screwtape Letters*, in which an older devil writes to his nephew, advising and instructing him how to keep one human soul, his 'patient', out of the clutches of 'The Enemy' – that is, God. He encourages the young devil to keep his patient weak, self-absorbed and confused: 'Do remember you are there to fuddle him. From the way some of you young fiends talk, anyone would suppose it was our job to *teach!*'[10]

In a time of quiet, name before God all those influences in your life which tend to harm rather than help. Call to mind the habits, relationships and preoccupations which lead you away from strength and self-knowledge, and perhaps turn you away from God. Confess them and lay them in God's hands, praying for the strength to resist them.

15 DECEMBER

Evil

The Supreme Being had a map of all creation which has been stolen from him by a gang of renegade employees. In the Fortress of Ultimate Darkness, Evil plots to steal the map for himself and so gain complete power over the universe. At the height of the last battle, Evil himself is destroyed by the Supreme Being: he is turned into a figure of black stone which then explodes. The Supreme Being, who resembles a kindly but strict headmaster, orders his minions to collect every last scattered piece of Evil, because even a tiny bit retains huge destructive power.

This scene, from the film, *Time Bandits*, reminds me of a fictional priest's description of the devil: 'He is without substance, breaking into a million pieces which worm their evil ways into the blood, into the soul.'[11]

In your prayers today, look at the world around you for those things which threaten love, peace and happiness. Bring before God the obvious evils and the headline-grabbing wickedness; remember too the bits of badness which insinuate themselves into everyday life. Name them and place them in his hands.

16 DECEMBER

Angel in the ironworks

Three men in robes and sandals are standing with a radiant, winged figure in the white heat of an industrial furnace. Around them are the gantries, spiral staircases and waste heaps of a modern ironworks; there is smoke, steam and a figure working above the furnace in protective clothing.

This striking scene, by the contemporary poet and painter Robert Wagner,[12] shows a modern interpretation of the story of Shadrach, Meshach and Abednego, who were thrown into the 'burning fiery furnace' by King Nebuchadnezzar as punishment for their refusal to worship his golden statue. An angel appeared with them in the furnace and protected them completely, so that 'the fire had not had any power over the bodies of those men; the hair of their heads was not singed, their tunics were not harmed, and not even the smell of fire came from them'.[13]

In your prayers today, remember the angel in the ironworks and bring before God those modern workplaces where his presence is needed. Remember the factories and offices, the shops and building sites which, to those who work there, may not feel like places for him.

17 DECEMBER

Tobias and the angel

Tobias is a young man who is faced with a difficult task: his father wants him to travel to a foreign country to reclaim his fortune, held there in trust for twenty years. Tobias is told to hire a trustworthy man from the marketplace as his guide:

> He went out and found the angel Raphael standing in front of him; but he did not perceive that he was an angel of God. Tobias said to him, 'Where do you come from, young man?' 'From your kindred, the Israelites,' he replied, 'and I have come here to work.'[14]

On their long journey they have many adventures, during which Raphael oversees Tobias' safety, finds him a wife, cures her of demonic possession and shows the young man how to cure his father's blindness. Finally his angelic guardian reveals the truth:

> I am Raphael, one of the seven angels who stand ready and enter before the glory of the Lord ... Do not be afraid; peace be with you. Bless God for evermore ... Bless him each and every day; sing his praises.[15]

In a time of quiet, reflect on this story from the Apocrypha. Consider the hands-on practicality of God's angel, who came to work; notice the focus on God's goodness and glory at the end. In your prayers today, open your eyes to God's work being carried out in the world, perhaps by unexpected or unrecognised people, and give thanks.

18 DECEMBER

Angel-song

> Yet with the woes of sin and strife
> the world has suffered long;
> beneath the angel-strain have rolled
> two thousand years of wrong;
> and man, at war with man, hears not
> the love-song which they bring:
> O hush the noise, ye men of strife,
> and hear the angels sing.[16]

The angels who sang of peace and goodwill at Christ's birth continue to sing, but we have drowned out their music. This powerful image suggests that if we could only tune in to the heavenly song, we could transmit to the world its message of love and peace.

In your prayers today, consider yourself as a channel through which God may pour his grace into the world. Try praying through this well-known prayer:

> Lord,
> make me an instrument of your peace.
> Where there is hatred, let me sow love.
> Where there is injury, pardon.
> Where there is doubt, faith.
> Where there is despair, hope.
> Where there is darkness, light.
> Where there is sadness, joy.[17]

19 DECEMBER
Oriel's Diary

This book by Robert Harrison is the diary of the Archangel Oriel, in which he tells the story of Jesus' life from his perspective. He is a kind of senior civil servant, overseeing a heaven run by a hierarchy of angels in the service of God. There is bureaucracy, paperwork and in-fighting (Gabriel is resented for getting the best jobs), as well as reflections on God's purpose for the world as the angels help him implement his plans. In preparing for Jesus' arrival, they are busy as messengers and guides; Oriel frets over the haphazard arrangements for the birth and, having seen the work of creation at first hand, struggles to comprehend *why* God wants to be born as one of us:

> And now, the One who held every atom in his grasp is no more than a clutch of watery cells in the midst of a teenage girl, in an obscure village, in a defeated nation, on one of the smaller planets that orbit an ordinary star, in an uneventful galaxy that turns on its little axis in that gassy cloud that is the Universe, which the Son himself made.
>
> Such smallness I can barely begin to imagine. This is Love.[18]

In a time of quiet, reflect on this passage, letting your mind grasp that familiar yet extraordinary truth: God became one of us. Rest in his presence and give thanks.

20 DECEMBER

Waiting

This period feels as if it is all about waiting. We are caught up in a whirl of Christmas preparations; children are eagerly anticipating Christmas morning; the Gospel stories of Advent remind us of a young mother awaiting her baby's birth while a whole nation looks for the coming of a new king, the Messiah.

In a time of prayer, remember before God all those who are waiting:

> remember the parents-to-be, waiting in anxiety and hope for their child to be born;
>
> remember the terminally ill, fearing death yet waiting to die;
>
> remember those caught up in violent conflicts, watching for news of their loved ones;
>
> remember the asylum-seeker, waiting for a judgement;
>
> remember the lonely, longing to find true love;
>
> remember the doctors and surgeons, waiting for a life-saving treatment to take effect;
>
> remember the addict, focused on her next fix, and the gambler, waiting for his big win;
>
> remember those close to you who are waiting.

Pray that they may know God's presence with them as they wait, and when their waiting is over.

21 DECEMBER
Waiting for Godot

Two characters, Estragon and Vladimir, spend the whole of this play on an almost bare stage, squabbling and debating, while they wait for the mysterious Godot. Repeatedly, Estragon suggests they leave, and Vladimir says they can't go anywhere:

> Estragon: Why not?
> Vladimir: We're waiting for Godot.
> Estragon: (*despairingly*) Ah![19]

This conversation recurs throughout, and they never leave – and Godot never turns up. The play paints an extraordinary picture of futility and despair, dramatising a blank existence from which *God*ot is always absent.

In a time of quiet, bring before God the times when you have felt that he is far away, and your days are merely ticking by; remember too those close to you who seem to be experiencing a similar 'dry spell' in their lives. Pray for refreshment and new hope that this time of waiting may be rewarded.

22 DECEMBER

The Stature of Waiting

This is the title of a wonderful book by W. H. Vanstone, in which he examines our modern experience of waiting. We are frequently exasperated by having no control over our own lives, being instead at the mercy of everything from traffic jams and cancelled trains to NHS waiting lists. Vanstone sees illness, sudden disability and unemployment as other forms of waiting, to which we react with frustration and despair.

He suggests that our experiences of waiting are made harder to bear by our assumption we are *supposed* to be masters of our own destiny – that 'human dignity is preserved only to the extent that man is active in the world, and initiates and creates and earns and achieves'. We hate being unable to manage for ourselves; relying on others makes us feel we are 'a burden' rather than a person. Vanstone challenges this by re-examining the Gospel accounts of Holy Week. He argues convincingly that the supreme moment of Christ's sacrifice happens not on the Cross but in the Garden of Gethsemane, when he puts himself in the hands of the soldiers and, in so doing, becomes not the God who is active in the world, teaching and healing, but the God who makes himself subject to the will of others. He stops *doing*, and allows everything to be *done to* him, including torture and crucifixion. He becomes 'The God Who Waits'.[20]

continued overleaf

In your prayers, bring before God your own frustration at having to wait. Know that his example teaches us that we live not only to be active, but also to be exposed and receptive to the world we inhabit. Listen to him in your waiting, and know that he has been there, too.

23 DECEMBER

The God who waits

In a poem called 'God-Forgotten', Thomas Hardy wrestled with his own doubts about a loving Creator. He imagines meeting God, who at first denies all knowledge of us:

> 'The Earth, sayest thou? The Human race?
> By me created? Sad its lot?
> Nay: I have no remembrance of such place:
> such world I fashioned not.'

The poet insists, and eventually God recalls, 'Some tiny sphere I built long back'. He believed his creation – a 'tainted ball' – had perished long ago, because he had heard nothing of its troubles.[21]

This frightening vision voices the doubts which can grip us all. But we can counter it with a single word: Jesus. The Incarnation of God as man reveals a God so deeply involved in his own creation that he became one of us – not to dominate and rule us but to make himself subject, for our sake, to the worst that humankind could do to him.

In your prayers, give thanks this Christmas for the vulnerable baby in the stable, whose living and dying bind us for ever to our loving God. That bond remains, whether we want it, scorn it or deny its existence. I'm reminded of the priest's response to the parishioner who said, 'I'm afraid my mother didn't believe in God.'

'Never mind,' replied the priest, 'he believed in her.'

24 DECEMBER

Christmas Eve

> What has come into being in him was life, and the life was the light of all people. The light shines in the darkness, and the darkness did not overcome it ... The true light, which enlightens everyone, was coming into the world.[22]

Today, take some time to step away from all the busy preparations for Christmas Day. Find a quiet place and simply light a candle; as you do so, say, 'The light of the world'.

Rest in the presence of the living God, in the indomitable light of his love.

25 DECEMBER

Christmas Day

Christmas Day in this vicar's household begins with Midnight Mass, which in practice means nobody gets to bed before two o'clock in the morning. Then it's an early start – about six o'clock – to prepare for the early Christmas Day service, which is followed by the mid-morning family service. Then lunch, and all the usual Christmas activities squeezed into the rest of the afternoon and evening. It makes me think of the daily prayer offices which form the backbone of monastic life and feature in the Catholic Books of Hours.[23] These are prayers throughout the day: Vigils at night, Lauds at daybreak, Terce at mid-morning, Sext at noon, None in the afternoon, Vespers in the evening and Compline at the end of the day.

Today's prayers follow this structure. Each line may be said at the appropriate time, or the whole prayer may be used in a time of quiet. Encompass this day in prayer, remembering that birth through which God came and lived among us:

Night	In this still, small hour of darkness, he is here.
Daybreak	As dawn lights the way, he is here.
Mid-morning	In my woken, working morning, he is here.
Noon	In the fullness of noon, he is here.

continued overleaf

Afternoon	In this afternoon's playing or perseverance, he is here.
Evening	In the tired time, as the light fades, he is here.
End of the day	At the end, when it is time to rest, he is here.
	Praise be to God, who is one with us today. Amen.

26 DECEMBER

Boxing Day

The presents have been unwrapped, the boxes opened, the food eaten and the wine drunk. After yesterday's festivities, today can feel a little flat. I find myself spending a lot of time clearing away the rubbish: the leftover food, the discarded wrapping paper and the empty crackers.

In a time of quiet, choose one of these discarded items as a focus for prayer. Take an empty box or a piece of torn wrapping paper and ask yourself: is this what I often end up offering to God – the leftover bits of myself and my time that have not been claimed by anyone else? Rest in God's presence and confess those times when this may have been true; pray that he might show you how to give your whole self. What could this mean for you?

27 DECEMBER

Pantomime

The Christmas pantomime is a seasonal treat, and much of our enjoyment lies in the familiarity of its rituals, from yelling, 'It's behind you!' to the sing-along and sweets. The following prayers have been inspired by pantomime traditions.

Clowns

My children were doubled up with laughter as they relived the slapstick comedy they had enjoyed in that evening's panto. The comedy double act, custard pies in hand, had teetered about the stage, *almost* taking aim at various characters until – of course – they bumped into one another and each landed a pie squarely in the other's face. SPLAT! Then they had mucked about with a bucket of water, and those of us sitting near the front of the stage had cringed every time they got ready to hurl it in our direction. Just when we thought we were safe, one tripped up the other, the bucket tipped, we braced ourselves for a soaking – and we were covered in a shower of glitter. The children hooted with delight and relief.

Clowning both fulfils our expectations (someone *will* end up with a pie in the face) and surprises us with the unexpected (Oooh! Glitter! But where did the water go?). In your prayers today, consider the capacity of life to surprise and delight you. Recall the times when your dearest hope was fulfilled or joy took you by surprise, and give thanks to God, from whom all good things come.

28 DECEMBER
Pantomime villain

The arrival of the pantomime villain is an unmistakable event. He or she traditionally appears on the left side of the stage, and the lighting darkens or turns a sinister shade of green. A puff of smoke, a drum roll, and there is the 'baddy' whom we greet with loud boos and hisses.

If evil always announced itself so clearly, the influences which harm us in our everyday lives would be much easier to spot. In a time of quiet, reflect on your own life and those close to you. Name those things which are causing discord, damage or pain; bring them to God in prayer and ask for the wisdom to know what to do, and the strength to do it.

29 DECEMBER
Principal boy

If the pantomime villain is exactly what he seems, then the same cannot be said for the 'goodies'. The principal boy is a woman in tights and the dame is a man in a dress: role-playing and disguise are at the heart of the pantomime.

In a time of quiet, consider the ways in which you play a role. We all have a family part to play, as parent, child or sibling; many of us have a working or caring role too. Think of the different parts you play: do they show the real you, or are some a disguise? Have some been imposed upon you? In your prayers today, pray for the strength to find and be the real you. Name before God the roles which conceal or deny who you really are, and ask for his help in turning them into better reflections of your true self – the self known and loved by God.

30 DECEMBER

The walk down

The traditional sing-along just before the end of the pantomime has a very practical purpose: it is there to give the principal characters time to change into their best costumes for the finale, known as the 'walk down'. A strict order is observed for this important panto ceremony, as each player in turn, from the least important to the hero, parades down the steps to receive his or her applause. The rest of the cast stands formally in attendance as each one gets his moment of recognition and appreciation.

In your prayers today, consider the importance of saying thank you. Name before God all those things for which, at the moment, you are especially grateful; pray too for the wisdom to know when thanks are due to others, and for the grace to show your appreciation.

31 DECEMBER

New Year's Eve

> Just as I am, though tossed about
> with many a conflict, many a doubt,
> fightings within, and fears without:
> O Lamb of God, I come.[24]

In your hands you hold the pages which have taken you through a year of praying. Today, look back and remember. You may recall painful and joyful times through which you prayed, or dark days when prayer was hard. One day you may have struggled to stay awake for an early prayer; another, you may have been too busy to concentrate. Perhaps you were blessed with a moment of epiphany or a new calling. Whatever your experiences have been, consider that you didn't come to prayer in your Sunday best, but as your everyday self. Today, praise the God who loves you like that, just as you are:

> Praise be to you, ever-loving Lord;
> your love takes me just as I am:
> a living patchwork of loving, dreaming,
> hoping, hurting, fearing, working,
>   playing and praying.
> You know all the pieces of me,
> the best and the worst of me,
> and yet your love enfolds me,
> as indeed I praise you – just as I am.
> Amen.

Seasonal Material

Shrove Tuesday

Whether it means pancake parties or Mardi Gras, this has traditionally been the day for celebrating before the austerity of Lent takes over. The word 'carnival' was coined for this day's festivities (it means, literally, 'leaving aside meat' for Lent). The great medieval carnivals were a liberation for the people: for one mad, colourful day, they were in charge and the traditional figures of authority – the kings, mayors and bishops – were exposed to mockery and general silliness. The modern Carnival Queen is a reminder of those original carnivals, when ordinary people took over and ran the show.

In the Gospels, Jesus promises a similar overturning of the social order. As a preparation for prayer, look at the story of the workers in the vineyard. The farmer hires workers at different stages during the day, but when the work is done he pays them all the same daily wage, regardless of whether they had slaved all day in the heat or turned up after tea. When the first workers complain, the farmer defends his right to be generous to all, and Jesus comments that it will be like this in the kingdom of heaven, too: 'So the last will be first, and the first will be last.'[1] In your prayers, take some time to reflect on this challenging message. Who has your sympathy in the story? What does it say about the generosity of God's love?

Ash Wednesday

There is a hauntingly lovely piece of music associated with this day. It is a setting of Psalm 51 composed by Gregorio Allegri in the early seventeenth century and it has a mysterious reputation. The story goes that it was only to be sung in the Sistine Chapel, and only at certain services, by order of the Pope. Breaking these rules – even by writing the music down – meant excommunication.

Appropriately for the start of Lent, Psalm 51 dwells on a sense of sinfulness and a longing for forgiveness. In its musical setting, low voices chant a confession while a single, plaintive voice soars above them, crying out for mercy with a sound of unearthly beauty. Today, take some time to read Psalm 51, which begins:

> Have mercy on me, O God,
> according to your steadfast love;
> according to your abundant mercy
> blot out my transgressions.
> Wash me thoroughly from my iniquity,
> and cleanse me from my sin.[2]

If you can, listen to the musical setting, known as Allegri's *Miserere*. Hold the Psalm in prayer and let it speak to you, as you consider those things in your own life and heart which you want to see washed away.

Mothering Sunday

> Jesus Christ who does good against evil is our true Mother – we have our being from him where the basis of motherhood begins, with all the sweet protection of love that accompanies it endlessly ...
>
> To the quality of motherhood belongs natural love, wisdom, and knowledge – and this is God.[3]

We are used to thinking of God the Father, but the fourteenth-century nun who wrote these words expresses beautifully the motherly quality of Christ's love for us. As Mother's Day falls this month, take time to reflect on your experience of a mother's love. Recall your own mother, perhaps with the help of old family photographs, and remember the ways she cared for you as a child. If you are a mother yourself, think about the love you share with your children. Can we use these experiences as a way of thinking about God? Our God, who is

> mothering her people,
> teaching them to walk,
> lifting weary toddlers,
> bending down to feed them.[4]

Palm Sunday
Offering

I remember a Palm Sunday service when we re-enacted Christ's entry into Jerusalem in the church itself. Instead of putting an offering of money in the collection plate, we were invited to offer something of our own and to cover the aisle not with palm leaves, but with whatever we had to hand – a coat, a scarf, a bag, a newspaper. A barefooted teenager, wearing white and carrying a large wooden cross over his shoulders, then walked over the carpet of offerings we had made and took the cross to the altar.

As a symbolic action, it was very powerful, but what I found most interesting was the debate it started in my head. What would I place on the floor for Jesus to walk on? My coat was quite new, and the floor looked a bit dusty... Besides, it had my mobile phone in the pocket and I didn't want that getting broken. My bag was full of old receipts and tissues – it would be embarrassing if those spilled out all over the aisle. So I settled for my scarf, because not a lot of harm could come to it.

In a time of quiet, imagine yourself in the same position: what would you lay down? Rest in God's presence and let your answer speak to you. Are there parts of your life that you resist offering to God because of embarrassment or uncertainty? Or fear of what might happen if you do? Do you give only that part of yourself which doesn't cost too much?

Monday of Holy Week
Overturning the tables

I recently had a vivid anxiety dream about a conference at which my husband had been asked to speak. I was worried he might tell some home truths and that this would get him into trouble. I dreamed of a grand hotel's dining room with tables laid for a feast, where all his fellow clergy and the bishops were seated and waiting for him to speak. He got to his feet and without saying a word, picked up a big bowl of cream-covered trifle and threw it straight at the bishop. After a stunned pause, the dining room erupted into a fierce and incredibly messy food fight.

One thing Jesus did during his week in Jerusalem was to cause similar havoc in the most holy of places. Finding the temple full of money-changers and market stalls, he pushed over their tables and scattered their wares, declaring that the temple should be a place of prayer, while coins rolled in all directions and doves flapped in panic above the chaos.[5]

In a time of quiet, consider the call to be a trifle-thrower and a table-turner. Look around you at your own life and the wider world and ask yourself: what needs to change? What disruption might be needed to make things better?

Tuesday of Holy Week
Lazarus

In front of the stone tomb, crowds of women are wailing in grief. Christ is weeping too as men strain to shift the stone which has hidden the body of his friend, Lazarus, for the last four days. The dark mouth of the tomb is revealed and the sudden smell of decay makes everyone cover their nose and mouth. Clearly shaken, Christ goes to the entrance and calls softly for Lazarus. After a breathless pause, a discoloured hand, wrapped in strips of linen, thrusts out into the light. Lazarus has come back from the dead.

In this film depiction of the raising of Lazarus,[6] the reality of several days in the tomb is brought home to us. It is a brutal reminder of what Christ is about to face and overcome between his crucifixion and resurrection.

In your prayers, bring before God all those for whom the reality of death is very close:

> pray for those in hospital, in hospices and at home
> who are nearing the end of their lives;
>
> pray for those who are victims of violence, accidents or disasters
> who suddenly know that they are about to die;
>
> pray for those whose diagnosis brings the prospect of death closer,
>
> and pray for all who care for the dying.

Wednesday of Holy Week
Anointing

Jesus is eating a meal with friends when one of the women close to him anoints his feet with spikenard, a richly perfumed oil. In a modern retelling of this story, the perfume becomes a powerful symbol of love and grace, given with unstoppable generosity. The woman kneeling at Jesus' feet has had to break the neck of the alabaster jar:

> There was no question of holding back any ointment now – everything was his. The creamy unguent poured out – over my hands, over Jesus' hair, down his face and over his clothes. The lavish smell hit me like a flash of fire.[7]

In a time of quiet, call to mind the abundance of God's gifts and give thanks:

> Giving Lord,
> you pour out your goodness into our
>   lives,
> drenching us with your love.
> Give us eyes to see your grace,
> even when it seems like nothing more
> than a trickle in the darkest of corners.
> May our hearts and minds be like
>   cupped hands,
> open to receive your grace
> and ready to let it spill into the world.
> Amen.

Maundy Thursday
Service

Imagine the scene: Jesus and the disciples have been in Jerusalem for less than a week, and everywhere he goes, jostling crowds follow him. Jerusalem is packed for the Festival of Passover – it must have been like Oxford Street on Christmas Eve – and the streets are full of dust and noise. Jesus is also attracting the attention of the authorities, and some of his friends worry that the net is closing in. Then it is time to celebrate Passover itself, and they need to find somewhere quiet to share this special meal. They arrive at what has been called 'a Jerusalem safe-house'[8] with their sandalled feet covered in sweat, dirt and the dust of the streets. Normally, a servant would wash a guest's feet, but to their astonishment, Jesus himself is rolling up his sleeves, wrapping a towel round his waist like an apron and fetching a bowl of water. In his hands he takes Peter's size tens, with their blisters and bunions, and carefully rinses and dries them.

Even though such an act of service speaks for itself, Jesus spells it out for the disciples:

> So if I, your Lord and Teacher, have washed your feet, you also ought to wash one another's feet. For I have set you an example, that you also should do as I have done to you.[9]

In a time of quiet, hold this scene in your imagination and ask God to speak to you through it. Ask how this is an example for you, in your life now. Ask, and listen.

Good Friday
Inhuman and degrading treatment

In recent years, the abuse of political prisoners has become big news: photographic evidence from Abu Ghraib prison led to the trials of young soldiers; governments have been accused by Amnesty International of 'outsourcing torture' and stories from Guantánamo Bay continue to horrify. The human rights movement has a term for it: 'inhuman and degrading treatment'. As Easter approaches, we remember events in the Middle East two millennia ago, when a young man was condemned by the superpower of his day to suffer similar treatment at the hands of his guards, before being executed on the cross.

In a time of quiet today, pray for all those who are in prison:

> those who have been rightly and wrongly convicted;
>
> those in prison without trial;
>
> those who are tortured and humiliated by their captors.
>
> Pray for relief from their suffering in body, mind and spirit,
> in the name of Christ who experienced their pain.

Easter Saturday
The Vigil

In recent years, there have been some extraordinary scenes of spontaneous vigils, held in response to a great disaster or loss. Think of the 11 September attacks, or the death of Princess Diana: huge, silent crowds waited with candles, flowers, photographs and messages; people held each other and wept.

In many churches tonight, a Vigil will be kept as we wait for Easter's new dawn. In your prayers today, remember Christ's words to his disciples in the Garden of Gethsemane: 'Remain here, and keep awake.'[10] Simply sit and watch and wait ...

Easter Sunday
Let there be light

> The true light, which enlightens everyone, was coming into the world ... The light shines in the darkness, and the darkness did not overcome it.[11]

The celebration of Easter begins with light: the dawn, sometimes a bonfire, and the light of the Paschal candle entering a dark church. On Easter Day the light of Life triumphs over the darkness of death which had engulfed Good Friday.

When you pray, light a candle in a darkened room and reflect on the power and beauty of that simple light. Bring to mind the dark places of the world and your own soul that need the blessing of Christ's true light; after each prayer intention, repeat the response:

> In all these dark places
> let there be light.[12]

Give thanks for the promise of Easter: the light still shines in the darkness, and the darkness does not overcome it.

Ascension

This is the day on which the resurrected Jesus was taken back up into heaven in front of his astonished disciples. It makes me think of a picture in a medieval manuscript which looks like something out of a comic: at the bottom of the frame, there are twelve upturned faces, each mouth an 'O' of surprise. There are some hands, waving and pointing – and dangling above them, at the very top of the picture, is a pair of feet.

This is a graphic illustration of how we often think of God: he is 'up there'. However, the Ascension marks the moment when Christ's transforming power and presence came to be shared among us all. In a time of quiet, dwell on the words which are attributed to St Patrick:

> Christ be with me, Christ within me,
> Christ behind me, Christ before me,
> Christ beside me, Christ to win me,
> Christ to comfort and restore me,
> Christ beneath me, Christ above me,
> Christ in quiet, Christ in danger,
> Christ in hearts of all that love me,
> Christ in mouth of friend and stranger.[13]

Pentecost

> Come, Holy Ghost, our souls inspire
> and lighten with celestial fire[14]

I love the words of this ancient hymn for Pentecost. What an invitation it makes, asking the Holy Spirit to inspire and lighten our souls with fire from heaven! That is what happened to the disciples on that first Pentecost, when tongues of flame appeared above their heads and their inspired words poured out of them in languages that their multiracial audience could understand. The flames of the Holy Spirit caught those who were listening, and started to spread like wildfire. I once saw a play which dramatised this moment spectacularly: the disciples were standing at the front of a raked stage, and behind them, seemingly above their heads, the darkness was suddenly split by a blast of flame, then another, and another. It was as if each man had become a human torch, ablaze with the Holy Spirit.[15]

Pentecost may seem to us a rather extreme event, and yet we can recognise that feeling of being inspired, 'fired up' with energy and enthusiasm. In a time of quiet, reflect on your experience of inspiration – or the lack of it – and pray again for the fire of the Holy Spirit to descend.

Trinity Sunday

> I bind unto myself today
> the strong name of the Trinity,
> by invocation of the same,
> the three in One, and One in three.[16]

Celtic Christianity has a strong sense of the three-personed nature of God and the distinctive qualities of Father, Son and Holy Spirit. In your prayers today, try focusing in turn on each person of the Trinity, perhaps using these words:

> Father, loving Lord,
> Maker and Mender,
> cradle me in the hollow of your hands;
> Son of God, living Word,
> Saviour, Brother, Friend,
> walk with me through this day
> and all my days;
> Spirit of God, leaping like flame
> above and between and within us all,
> ignite me, enthuse and inspire me
> to do your will.
> Amen.

Father's Day

My dad taught me how to ride a bike. I remember wobbling along without my stabilisers, with Dad's hand on the back of the saddle and his reassuring voice in my ear. I remember that thrilling moment when I started to pedal more confidently, not quite sure whether he was still holding on. When I tried to look back and swerved, Dad's hand was there again, firmly gripping the saddle and holding the bike upright. Then I had another go and cycled in a sure, swift line to the bottom of the garden. I turned and saw that this time, I had been doing it all by myself, but that my daddy had been watching all the way and was cheering by the back door.

From the moment a man becomes a father, he is shown the lesson that all parents must eventually learn, and learn with difficulty: that parenting, like teaching bike-riding, is all about holding on and letting go. Once a child is conceived, a father is given a supporting role in the unfolding drama of new life. Throughout pregnancy, birth and breastfeeding, his job is to support, help and provide for both mother and baby, but he himself can't turn in the womb, push or learn how to feed. As his children grow, they need both the freedom to find their own way, and the confidence that their parents' love will never abandon them.

In your prayers today, reflect on your experience of a father's love. Remember your own dad, and the childhood moments you recall sharing. If you are a father yourself, consider how you love your children. Give thanks for fathers, and thank God, too, for his fatherly love and care. As we free-wheel into the future, his anxious love watches over us and his hand is close by, ready to help us steer or catch us when we fall.

Acknowledgements

The Publishers wish to thank all those who have given their permission to reproduce copyright material in this publication.

Every effort has been made to trace the owners of copyright material and we hope that no copyright has been infringed. Pardon is sought and apology made if the contrary be the case, and a correction will be made in any reprint of this book.

NRSV

Except where indicated in the Sources section, Scripture quotations are from the *New Revised Standard Version Bible*, copyright © 1989, by the Division of Christian Education of the National Council of the Churches of Christ in the USA, and are used by permission. All rights reserved.

NIV

Scripture quotations taken from the *Holy Bible, New International Version*. Copyright © 1973, 1978, 1984 by International Bible Society. Used by permission of Hodder & Stoughton, a member of the Hodder Headline Group. All rights reserved. 'NIV' is a trademark of International Bible Society. UK trademark number 1448790.

REB

From *Revised English Bible* © Oxford University Press and Cambridge University Press 1989.

Common Worship

The Church of England's adapted form of the *Revised Common Lectionary*, published as the Principal Service Lectionary in *Common Worship: Services and Prayers for the Church of England*, the Second and Third Service Lectionaries and the *Common Worship* Calendar, also published in the same publication are copyright © The Archbishops' Council of the Church of England, 1995, 1997.

Book of Common Prayer

The Book of Common Prayer – Rights in *The Book of Common Prayer* are vested in the Crown, and administered by the Crown's patentee, Cambridge University Press.

Roman Missal

Excerpts
Excerpts from the English translation of *The Roman Missal* © 1973, International Committee on English in the Liturgy, Inc. All rights reserved.

Further copyright information can be found within the Sources section.

Sources

Introduction

[1] Alan Richardson on the theology of prayer, ed. A. Richardson & J. Bowden, *A New Dictionary of Christian Theology*, SCM Press, 1983.

January

[1] Ann Lewin, *Watching for the Kingfisher*, Inspire imprint of Methodist Publishing House, 2004.
[2] Italics from source unknown, *The SPCK Book of Christian Prayer*, SPCK, 1995, p. 243.
[3] Mary Hoffman, *Three Wise Women*, Frances Lincoln, 1999.
[4] *Ibid.*
[5] Matthew 25:1-13; 18:10-14; 25:14-30; 20:1-16; Mark 4:2-9; Matthew 18:23-35.
[6] Mary Hoffman, *Three Wise Women*, Frances Lincoln, 1999.
[7] Sam Gerring in Scott Rice, *It Was A Dark and Stormy Night*, Friday Books, 2007.
[8] Matthew 18:3, 4.
[9] Helen Fielding, *Bridget Jones's Diary*, Picador, 1996.
[10] Ethan Coen and Joel Coen, *O Brother, Where Art Thou?*, Touchstone/Universal, 2000.
[11] Muslihuddin Sadi (1184–1291).
[12] Yann Martel, *Life of Pi*, Canongate Books, 2002, p. 135.
[13] John 4:14.
[14] Harry Smart, *Fool's Pardon*, Faber & Faber, 1995.
[15] My translation, from a cartoon by Sempé in *Vaguement Compétitif*, Editions Denoël, Paris, 1985.
[16] Psalm 139:14.
[17] Acts 9:1-22.
[18] Colin Thubron, *Emperor*, William Heinemann, 1978.
[19] David Koepp, *Spider-Man*, Columbia Pictures, 2002.
[20] 2 Corinthians 12:9, 10.

February

[1] Luke 2:22-40.
[2] Genesis 2:19, 20.
[3] Mary Stevenson, 'Footprints in the Sand', © 1984 Mary Stevenson.
[4] W. B. Yeats, 'Aedh Wishes for the Cloths of Heaven', *The Wind Among the Reeds*, 1899.
[5] Revd Stephen Lowe, *Church Times*, 4 April 2008.
[6] Matthew 11:28.

[7] Kathy Galloway, Iona Community, *The SPCK Book of Christian Prayer*, SPCK, 1995, p. 252.
[8] *Common Worship*, Church House Publishing; © The Archbishops' Council, 2000.
[9] Mark Andrus and James L. Brooks, As *Good As It Gets*, TriStar Pictures, 1997.
[10] Jean Vanier, *Befriending the Stranger*, Darton, Longman & Todd, 2005, p. 59 and Preface, p. vii.
[11] John Wesley, *Sermons*, no. xciii.
[12] Psalm 51:7.
[13] Psalm 51:10.
[14] Mark 7:14-23.
[15] Fr Kevin Morris.
[16] *Man Stroke Woman*, Season 1, episode 4, BBC TV.
[17] Dylan Thomas, *Miscellany One*, J. M. Dent & Sons Ltd, 1963.
[18] John Macleod Crum, 'Now the green blade riseth', © Oxford University Press, 1928.

March

[1] Garrison Keillor, *We Are Still Married*, Viking Penguin, 1989.
[2] Psalm 22:14, 15.
[3] Jeffrey Boam (screenplay), *Indiana Jones and the Last Crusade*, Lucasfilm/Paramount, 1989.
[4] Richard LaGravenese, *The Fisher King*, Columbia Pictures, 1991.
[5] Traditional.
[6] 1 Corinthians 13:4, 7.
[7] Exodus 16:31.
[8] Simon Armitage, *Killing Time*, Faber & Faber, 1999.
[9] J. Edmeston (1791–1867), 'Lead us, heavenly Father, lead us'.
[10] 'St Patrick's Breastplate', ascribed to St Patrick (c.372–466), tr. Mrs C. F. Alexander (1818–95).
[11] 'Mensa' (Ethiopia) collected by Desmond Tutu in *An African Prayer Book*, Hodder & Stoughton, 1996, p. 96.
[12] Glynn Gorick, 'Sunlight Harvesting', 1993.
[13] 'St Patrick's Breastplate', ascribed to St Patrick, (c.372–466), tr. Mrs C. F. Alexander (1818–1895).
[14] David Adam, *The Eye of the Eagle*, Triangle SPCK, 1990, pp. 11, 12.
[15] *Ibid.* p. 11.
[16] Dennis Potter, in a *Without Walls* Special, LWT for Channel 4, 1994.
[17] Anonymous, *Primary Colors*, Chatto & Windus, 1996, p. 4.
[18] Donald Rumsfeld, US Defense Secretary.
[19] Stephen Fry, Foreword, *The Book Of General Ignorance*, Faber & Faber, 2006, pp. xiii, iv.
[20] John 10:10 (REB).
[21] James Runcie, *The Colour of Heaven*, HarperCollins, 2003, pp. 278-9, 285.

April

[1] Greg Garcia (creator), *My Name is Earl*, Twentieth Century Fox.
[2] Joy Division, 'Love Will Tear Us Apart', Factory Records FAC 23.
[3] James, 'Sit Down', Rough Trade/Mercury.
[4] New Order, 'Blue Monday', Factory Records FAC 73-7.
[5] Oasis, 'Wonderwall', Creation Records.
[6] Alan Bennett, *The Clothes They Stood Up In*, Profile Books, 1998, pp. 45, 46.
[7] Kathy Galloway, The Iona Community, *The Pattern of Our Days*, Wild Goose Publications, 1996, p. 29.
[8] Margaret Atwood, *Oryx and Crake*, Bloomsbury, 2003.
[9] Christine Odell, *Companion to the Revised Lectionary*, Epworth Press, 1998, p. 103.
[10] Appeal leaflet from Practical Action.
[11] Luke 15:11-32.
[12] Mark 10:21, 22.
[13] Juliet Stevenson in Carol Rutter's *Clamorous Voices*, The Women's Press, 1988.
[14] Ecclesiastes 3:1-8.
[15] John 14:6.
[16] Douglas Adams, *The Hitchhiker's Guide to the Galaxy*, Pan Books, 1979, p. 51.
[17] John Milton (1608–1674), Sonnet xvi, 'On His Blindness'.
[18] Luke 10:42.
[19] C. M. Noel (1817–1877), 'At the name of Jesus'.
[20] Hebrews 12:1 (NIV).

May

[1] Edwin Hatch (1835–1889), 'Breathe on me, Breath of God'.
[2] Peter Mayle, *A Year in Provence*, Penguin Books, 1989.
[3] Douglas Adams, *So long, and thanks for all the fish*, Pan Books, 1984, p.15.
[4] Peter Høeg, *Miss Smilla's Feeling for Snow*, HarperCollins, 1993, p. 410.
[5] My translation, *The Cloud of Unknowing*, l.288-296.
[6] Genesis 11:5-8.
[7] Acts 2:4-8, 11-13.
[8] Brian Friel, *Translations*, Faber & Faber, 1981, pp. 35, 43.
[9] J. G. Whittier (1807–1892), 'Dear Lord and Father of mankind'.
[10] Aaron Sorkin (creator), *The West Wing*, Warner Bros.
[11] Hugh Whitemore, *Breaking the Code*, Amber Lane Press, 1987.
[12] Ezekiel 37:7-10.
[13] John Donne (c. 1572–1631) *Holy Sonnet X*.
[14] Julie Miller, 'Broken Things', Hightone Records, 1999.
[15] Exodus 14 and 15.
[16] Bruce Chatwin, *The Songlines*, Jonathan Cape, 1987, pp. 14-16.
[17] Show of Hands, 'Roots', *Roots: The Best of Show of Hands*, HANDSONMUSIC.
[18] A. A. Milne, *The House at Pooh Corner*, 1928, copyright under the Berne Convention.
[19] Jim Cotter, '"Humming" and Patient Attentiveness', in *How I Pray*, ed. John Wilkins, Darton, Longman & Todd, 1993, p. 29.

June

1. Garrison Keillor, *Leaving Home*, Faber & Faber, 1988, p. 23.
2. W. C. Sellar and R. J. Yeatman, *1066 And All That*, Methuen, 1930, p. 24.
3. J. S. B. Monsell (1811–1875), 'O worship the Lord in the beauty of holiness'.
4. Scott Buck, *Rome*, Season 2 episode 19, HBO.
5. Kathy Galloway (ed.) The Iona Community, *The Pattern of Our Days*, Wild Goose Publications, 1996, p. 164.
6. A Commination, *The Book of Common Prayer*.
7. George du Maurier, 'True Humility', *Punch*, 9 November 1895.
8. Traditional Irish blessing.
9. From Trustees for Methodist Church Purposes, *The Methodist Worship Book*, Methodist Publishing House, 1999, p. 504.
10. From a Celtic Benediction (this and the lines which head the next four days' prayers).
11. © Ateliers et Presses de Taizé, F-71250 Taizé Communauté.
12. John V. Taylor, *The Go-Between God*, SCM Press, 1972, p. 7.
13. Psalm 23:1-3.
14. Michael Powell and Emeric Pressburger, *A Matter of Life and Death*, Universal Pictures, 1947.
15. *The Book of Common Prayer*, the Second Collect, Order for Evening Prayer.
16. *Common Worship*, Church House Publishing, © The Archbishops' Council, 2000.
17. Ariel Dorfman, *Death and the Maiden*, Nick Hern Books, 1991.
18. Philip Pullman, *Northern Lights*, Scholastic, 1995, p. 151.
19. *Ibid*. p. 152.
20. C. S. Lewis, *The Screwtape Letters*, Geoffrey Bles, 1942, p. 25.
21. John 8:32.
22. From the Book of Tobit 8:8 (Vulgate), quoted in the 'Blessing for Engaged Couples', Sean Finnegan (compiler), *Consecrations, Blessings and Prayers*, The Canterbury Press, 2005, p. 58.
23. Ali Smith, Girl Meets Boy, Canongate Books, 2007, p. 81.
24. *Man Stroke Woman*, Season 1, episode 4, BBC TV.

July

1. Daniel L. Schutte, 'I the Lord of Sea and Sky', © Daniel L. Schutte and New Dawn Music, 1981.
2. United States Declaration of Independence, 1776.
3. Spiritual (traditional).
4. Evelyn Waugh, *A Handful of Dust*, Chapman & Hall, 1934.
5. Oliver Wendell Holmes (1809–1894).
6. Matthew 6:28, 29.
7. Psalm 51:10.
8. William Shakespeare, *Hamlet*, Act 4, scene 5, l. 173-5.
9. Satchell Paige, US baseball player (1906–1982).
10. Ephesians 3:17-19 (NIV).
11. The English translation of *The Roman Missal*, © 1973, ICEL, HarperCollins *Religious*, 1984, p. 30.

12. David J. Evans, 'Be still, for the presence of the Lord', © 1986 Thankyou Music.
13. Sylvia Plath, 'Insomniac', ed. Ted Hughes, *Sylvia Plath's Selected Poems*, Faber & Faber, 1985.
14. *The Catherine Tate Show*, BBC TV.
15. Seán Finnegan (compiler), *A Book of Hours and other Catholic Devotions*, The Canterbury Press, Norwich, 1998, p. 20.
16. Tim Rice and Andrew Lloyd-Webber, *Joseph and the Amazing Technicolor Dreamcoat*, Novello, 1968. © 1969 The Really Useful Group Ltd.
17. Phillips Brooks (1835–1893), 'O little town of Bethlehem'.
18. William Shakespeare, *Macbeth*, Act 2, scene 2, l.34-9.

August

1. R. S. Thomas, 'Tidal', *Mass for Hard Times*, Bloodaxe Books, 1992.
2. 1 Thessalonians 5:16-18.
3. Iris Murdoch, *The Unicorn*, Chatto & Windus, 1963, p. 32.
4. Mark 6:47-51.
5. Walter Brueggemann, *Inscribing the Text*, Augsburg Fortress, 2004, p. 56.
6. 'St Patrick's Breastplate', ascribed to St Patrick, c.372–466, tr. Mrs C. F. Alexander (1818–1895).
7. St Teresa of Ávila (1515–1582).
8. Pam Ayres, 'With These Hands', *With These Hands*, Weidenfeld and Nicolson, 1997.
9. Jonathan Jones, *Guardian*, 17 February 2005.
10. Psalm 46:10.
11. Hans Feibusch, 'The Trinity in Glory', 1966.
12. Jonathan Swift (1667–1745), *A Modest Proposal*.
13. G. Chapman, J. Cleese, T. Gilliam, E. Idle, T. Jones, M. Palin, *Monty Python's Life of Brian*, HandMade Films, 1979.
14. Genesis 17:17.
15. *Ibid.* 18:12-15.
16. Joyce Grenfell, various monologues.
17. *The Book of Common Prayer*, The Third Collect for Evening Prayer, p. 24.
18. Ted Elliott and Terry Rossio, *Pirates of the Caribbean*, Walt Disney, 2003.
19. Stevie Smith, *The Collected Poems of Stevie Smith*, Penguin, 1972.

September

1. H. Alford, (1810–1871), 'Come, ye thankful people, come'.
2. Ray Galton, Alan Simpson, *The Rebel*, ABPC, 1961.
3. Margaret Atwood, *Cat's Eye*, Bloomsbury Publishing, 1989, p. 120.
4. My translation, 'The Dream of the Rood'.
5. See Mark 2:23–3:6; 7:1-23 and 11:12-21.
6. My translation, 'The Seafarer'.
7. Walter Skeat (ed.), *Aelfric's Lives of Saints*, Early English Text Society for OUP, 1966.
8. Simon Armitage (tr.), *Sir Gawain and the Green Knight*, Faber & Faber Ltd, 2007.
9. Isaiah 11:6, 9.
10. Sebastian Faulks, *Birdsong*, Hutchinson, 1993, p. 190.
11. Suzy Bogguss, 'Letting Go', *Aces*, Liberty, 1991.

October

1. Eleanor Farjeon, 'Morning has broken', © David Higham Associates Ltd, London.
2. Bede, *A History of the English Church and People*, translated by Leo Sherley-Price, Penguin, 1968, p. 127.
3. Gary Russell, *Dr Who: The Encyclopedia*, BBC Books, 2007, p. 168.
4. Robert Frost, 'The Road Not Taken', *Mountain Interval*, Holt, 1916.
5. Romans 8:38, 39.
6. Luke 10:38-42.
7. Francis Thompson (1859–1907), 'The Hound of Heaven'.
8. Margaret Wise Brown, *The Runaway Bunny*, HarperFestival, 2001.
9. Psalm 139:1, 2, 5-7, 9, 10.
10. Margaret Thatcher, talking to *Women's Own* magazine, 31 October 1987.
11. Paul Wotton, *My Journey – The First Ten Years*, Argyle Media Productions, 2004. p. 65.
12. Paul Wotton, quoting team-mate Micky Heathcote, *ibid*. p. 119.
13. Quoted by CNN.com/europe, 20 May 2008.
14. J. R. R. Tolkein, *The Hobbit*, George Allen & Unwin, 1937, chapter XIV.
15. J. K. Rowling, Harry Potter and the Prisoner of Azkaban, Bloomsbury Publishing, 1999, p. 66.
16. Craig Weatherhill and Paul Devereux, *Myths and Legends of Cornwall*, Sigma Leisure, 1994, p. 85.
17. Anon., Cornish.

November

[1] W. H. Auden, 'Stop all the clocks', *W. H. Auden Collected Poems*, Faber & Faber Ltd, 1976.
[2] A. S. Byatt, *Possession*, Chatto & Windus, 1990.
[3] Anna Maria Murphy, *What Girls Need*, Oberon Books, 2005.
[4] 1 Kings 3:16-28.
[5] Matthew 5:6.
[6] Quoted by Vikram Dodd in the *Guardian*, Friday 10 August 2007.
[7] Matthew 18:23-27.
[8] Matthew 18:28-30.
[9] William Shakespeare, *The Merchant of Venice*, Act 3, scene 3.
[10] John Robinson, *Honest to God*, SCM Press, 1963, pp. 1-6.
[11] Paul Tillich, *The Shaking of the Foundations*, 1949, quoted *ibid*. p. 9.
[12] Sarum Missal (1555).
[13] My translation, Jean Racine (1639–99), *Cantique de Jean Racine*.
[14] Olivia Sanders, *I It Am*, 1992, featured in John Wilkins (ed.), *How I Pray*, Darton, Longman & Todd, 1993.
[15] John 19:21, 22.
[16] Graham Kendrick, 'The Servant King', © 1983 Thankyou Music.
[17] Luke 11:2-4.
[18] John 10:11.
[19] Ezekiel 34:16.
[20] John 1:1-4.
[21] Wild Goose Resource Group, *Present on Earth*, Wild Goose Publications, 2002, p. 60.
[22] John 14:6.
[23] Genesis 1:1-4.
[24] Matthew Arnold (1822–88), 'Dover Beach'.
[25] John 8:12.

December

[1] Isaiah 40:3.
[2] Wild Goose Resource Group, *Cloth for the Cradle*, Wild Goose Publications, 1997, pp. 74, 75.
[3] Traditional saying (US).
[4] Joanne Harris, *Chocolat*, Doubleday, 1999, p. 33.
[5] William Hughes Mearns, 'Antigonish', 1922.
[6] John Kander and Fred Ebb, 'Mr Cellophane', *Chicago*, Warner Chappell North America Ltd,1975.
[7] Christina Rossetti (1830–1894), 'In the bleak midwinter'.
[8] Bob Hartman, illustrations by Jessica Curtis, *Angels, Angels All Around*, Lion Publishing, 1995.
[9] E.g. Genesis 16; Numbers 22; 1 Kings 19:4-9; Daniel 3; 6; Luke 1:26-38; 2:8-14; Matthew 2:13-15; 28:1-10.
[10] C. S. Lewis, *The Screwtape Letters*, Geoffrey Bles, 1942, p. 13.
[11] Joanne Harris, *Chocolat*, Doubleday, 1999, p. 34.
[12] Robert Wagner, 'The Burning Fiery Furnace' (1989).

13 Daniel 3:27.
14 Tobit 5:4, 5.
15 Tobit 12:15-18.
16 E. H. Sears (1810–76), 'It Came Upon a Midnight Clear'.
17 Attributed to Francis of Assisi (1181–1226).
18 Robert Harrison, *Oriel's Diary*, Scripture Union, 2002, p. 11.
19 Samuel Beckett, *Waiting for Godot*, Faber & Faber, 1965.
20 W. H. Vanstone, *The Stature of Waiting*, Darton, Longman & Todd, 1982, pp. 110, 88, 112.
21 Thomas Hardy (1840–1928), 'God-Forgotten'.
22 John 1:3-5, 9.
23 E.g. Seán Finnegan (compiler), *A Book of Hours and other Catholic Devotions*, The Canterbury Press Norwich, 1998.
24 Charlotte Elliott (1789–1871), 'Just as I am'.

Seasonal Material

1 Matthew 20:16.
2 Psalm 51:1, 2.
3 Father John-Julian OJN (tr.), *A Lesson of Love: The Revelations of Julian of Norwich*, Darton, Longman & Todd, 1988, pp. 154, 158.
4 Brian Wren, *Piece Together Praise*, Stainer & Bell Ltd, 1996.
5 Matthew 21:12-14.
6 *The Last Temptation of Christ*, Cineplex-Odeon Films/Universal, 1988.
7 Margaret Hebblethwaite, *Six New Gospels*, Geoffrey Chapman, 1994, p. 105.
8 Ched Myers, Greenbelt Festival, 2004.
9 John 13:14, 15.
10 Mark 14:34.
11 John 1:9, 5.
12 Rev. Marion Hinks.
13 'St Patrick's Breastplate', ascribed to St Patrick, c.372–466, tr. Mrs C. F. Alexander (1818-1895).
14 J. Cosin (1594–1672), after R. Maurus (c.776–856), 'Come, Holy Ghost'.
15 *The Mysteries*, Spier Festival Company, 2001.
16 'St Patrick's Breastplate', ascribed to St Patrick, c.372–466, tr. Mrs C. F. Alexander (1818–1895).

www.ingramcontent.com/pod-product-compliance
Lightning Source LLC
Chambersburg PA
CBHW020348080526
44584CB00014B/936